VALERIAN AND

MW00807764

THE LIVING WEAPONS

J.-C. MÉZIÈRES AND P. CHRISTIN
COLOURS: E. TRANLÉ

9th CINEBOOK
The 9th Art Publisher

Original title: Valerian – Les Armes Vivantes
Original edition: © Dargaud Paris, 1990 by Christin, Mezières & Tranlé
www.dargaud.com
All rights reserved
English translation: © 2016 Cinebook Ltd
Translator: Jerome Saincantin
Lettering and text layout: Design Amorandi
Printed in Spain by EGEDSA
This edition first published in Great Britain in 2016 by
Cinebook Ltd
56 Beech Avenue
Canterbury, Kent
CT4 7TA
www.cinebook.com
A CIP catalogue record for this book
is available from the British Library
ISBN 978-1-84918-319-2

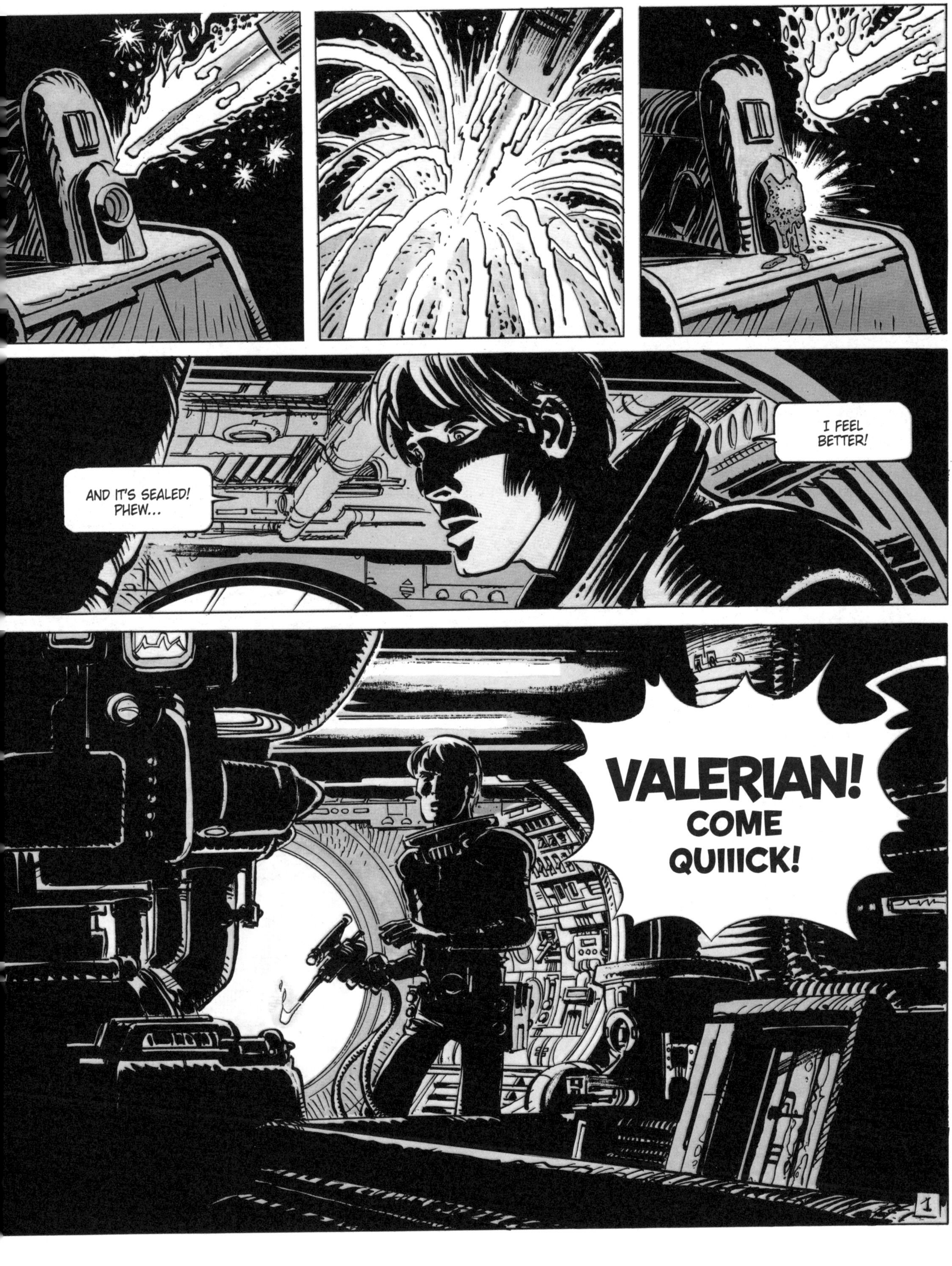
I FEEL BETTER!
AND IT'S SEALED! PHEW...
VALERIAN! COME QUIIICK!
1

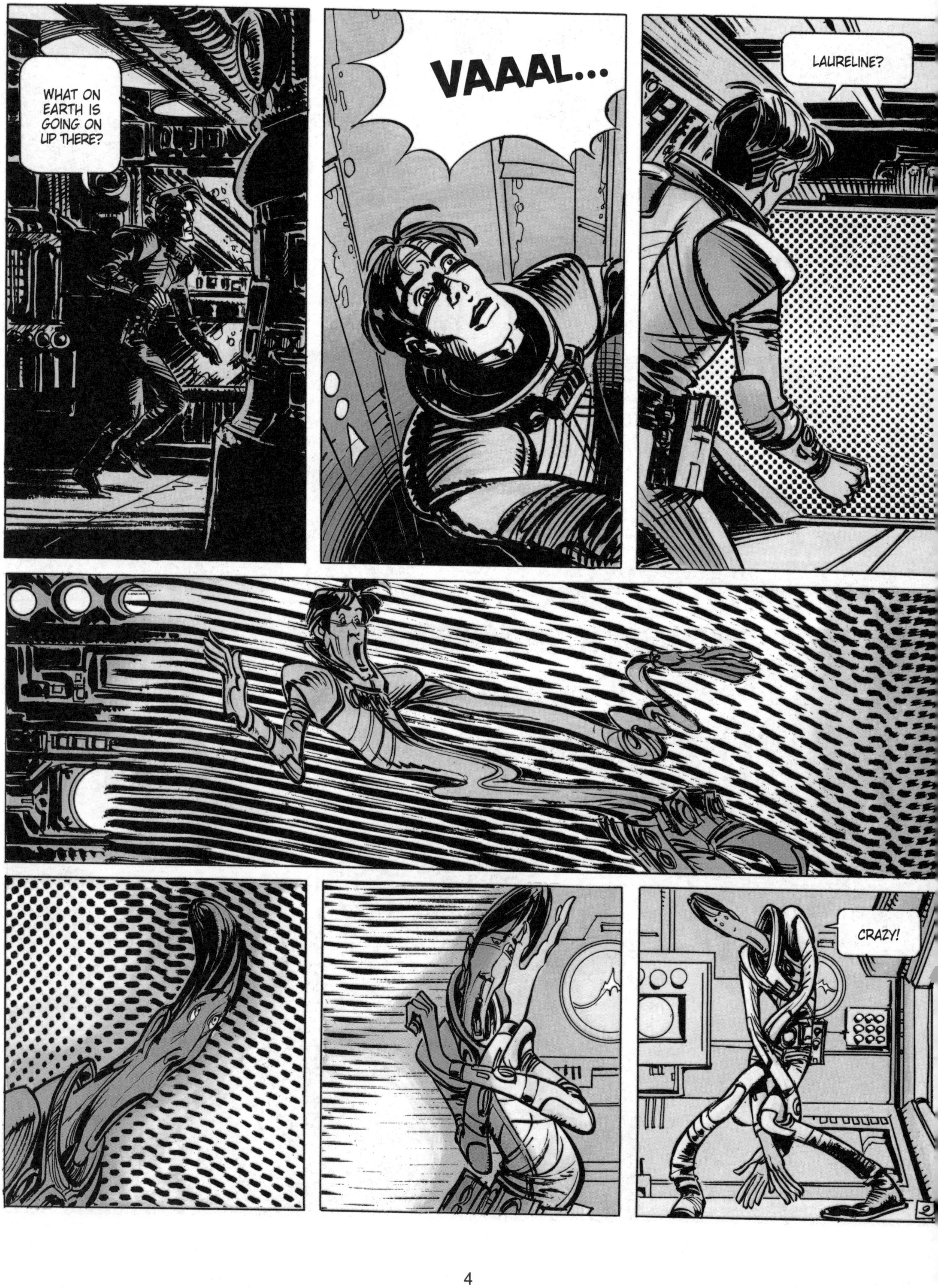
WHAT ON EARTH IS GOING ON UP THERE?
VAAAL...
LAURELINE?
CRAZY!

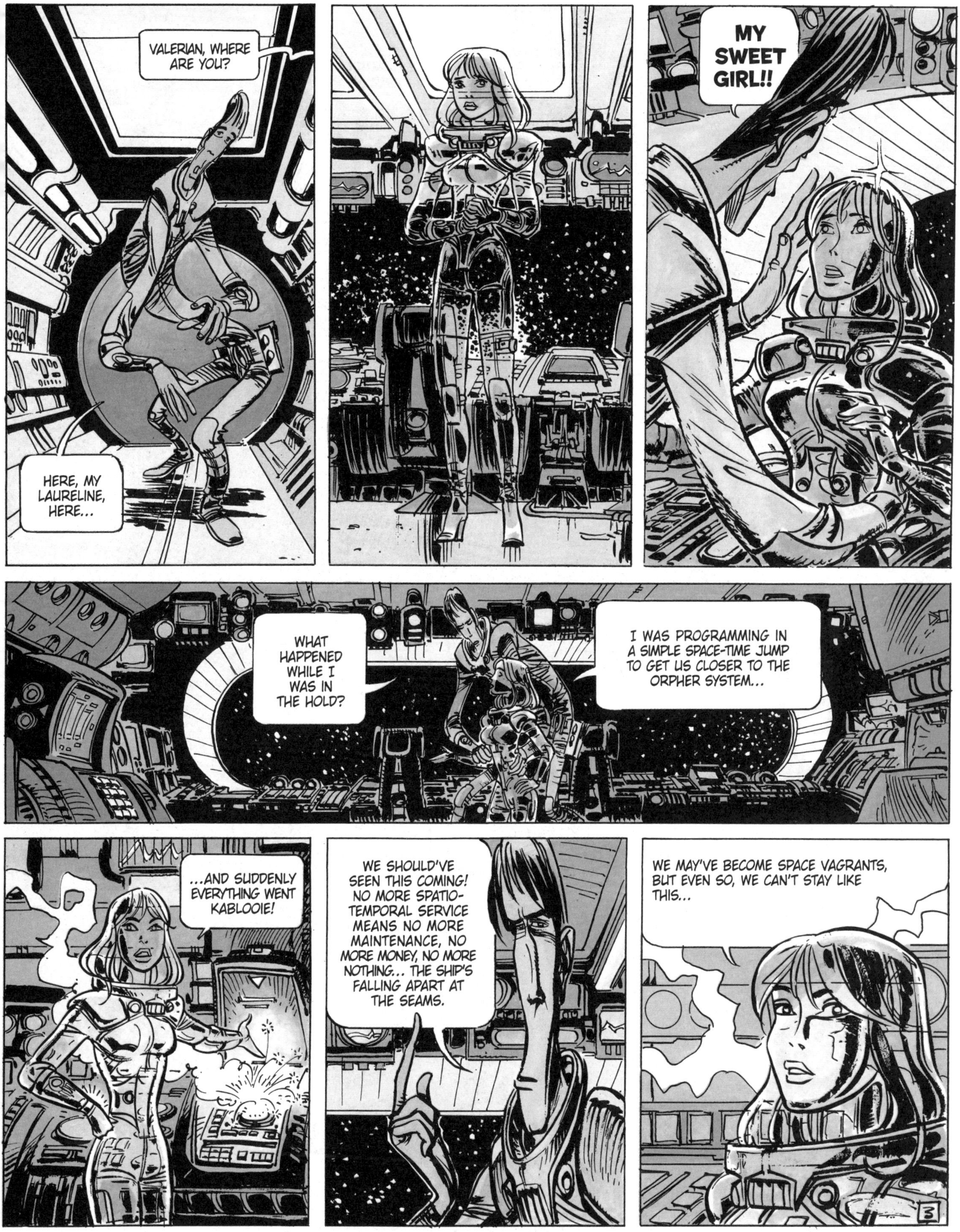
VALERIAN, WHERE ARE YOU?
HERE, MY LAURELINE, HERE...
MY SWEET GIRL!!
WHAT HAPPENED WHILE I WAS IN THE HOLD?
I WAS PROGRAMMING IN A SIMPLE SPACE-TIME JUMP TO GET US CLOSER TO THE ORPHER SYSTEM...
...AND SUDDENLY EVERYTHING WENT KABLOOIE!
WE SHOULD'VE SEEN THIS COMING! NO MORE SPATIO-TEMPORAL SERVICE MEANS NO MORE MAINTENANCE, NO MORE MONEY, NO MORE NOTHING... THE SHIP'S FALLING APART AT THE SEAMS.
WE MAY'VE BECOME SPACE VAGRANTS, BUT EVEN SO, WE CAN'T STAY LIKE THIS...
3

THERE'S A BACKUP SYSTEM... HASN'T BEEN USED IN YEARS...

...AND IT'S PRETTY BARE-BONES TOO! BUT IT SHOULD LET US ATTEMPT ANOTHER JUMP...

A JUMP TO WHERE?

HEH! SINCE WE HAVE NO IDEA WHERE WE ARE NOW ... NOT A CLUE!

THE MAIN THING IS TO RESTORE OUR OWN PHYSICAL INTEGRITY.

LET'S RISK IT. GO!

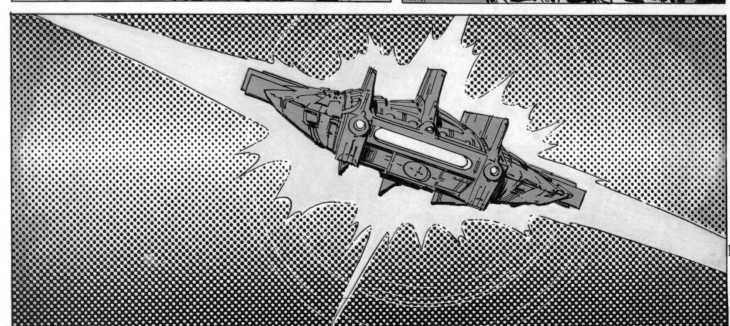

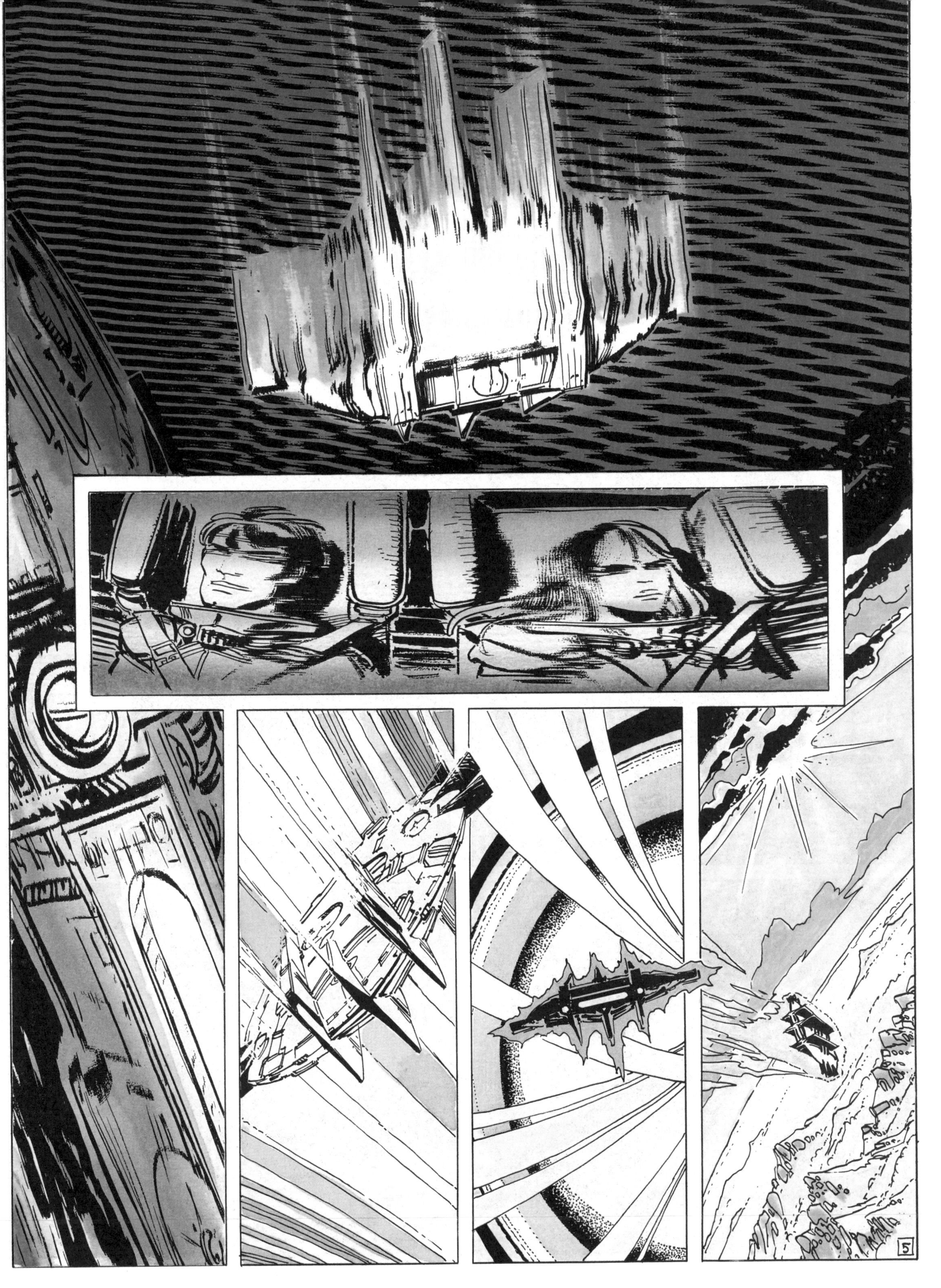
5

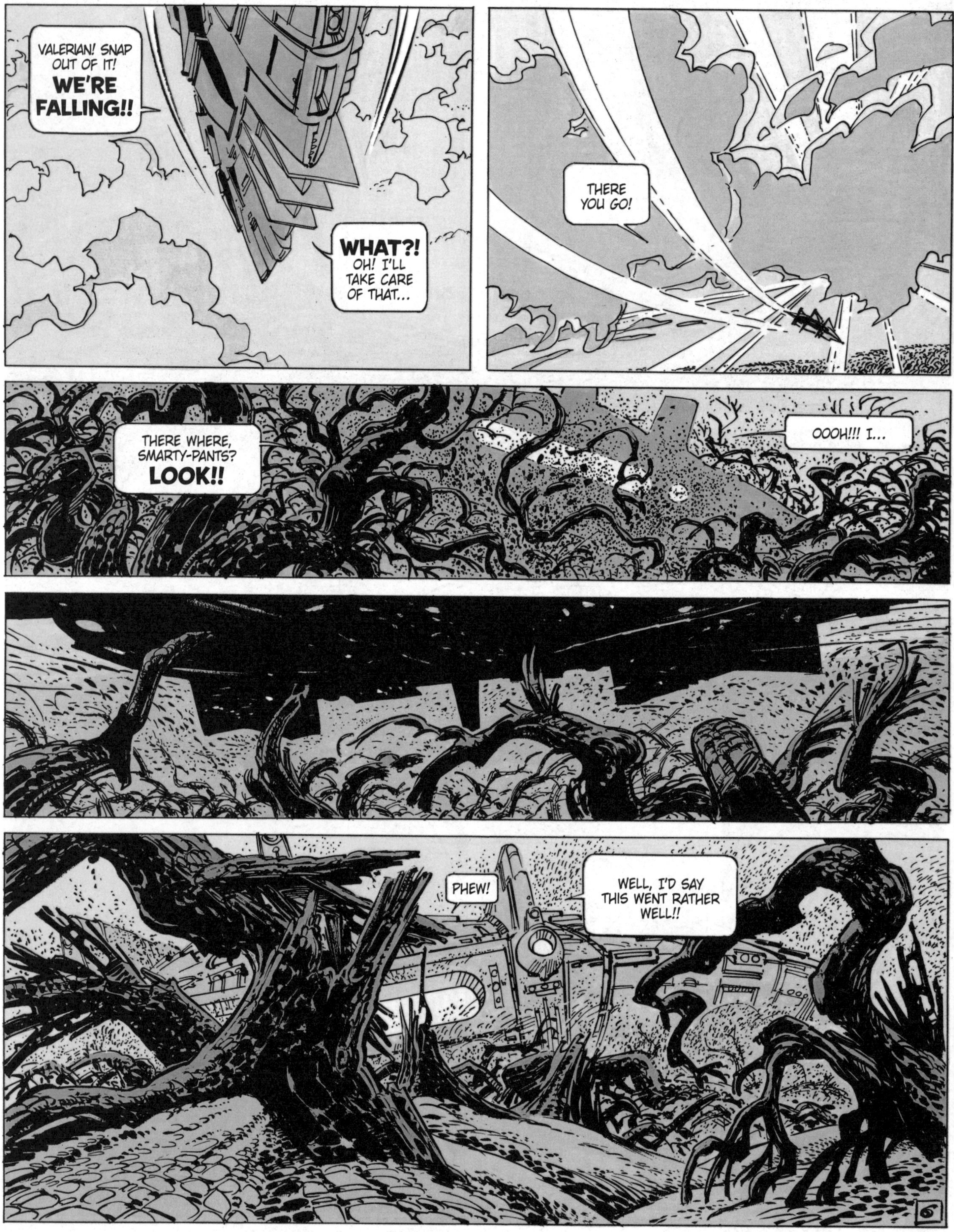
VALERIAN! SNAP OUT OF IT! WE'RE FALLING!!
WHAT?! OH! I'LL TAKE CARE OF THAT...
THERE YOU GO!
THERE WHERE, SMARTY-PANTS? LOOK!!
OOOH!!! I...
PHEW!
WELL, I'D SAY THIS WENT RATHER WELL!!

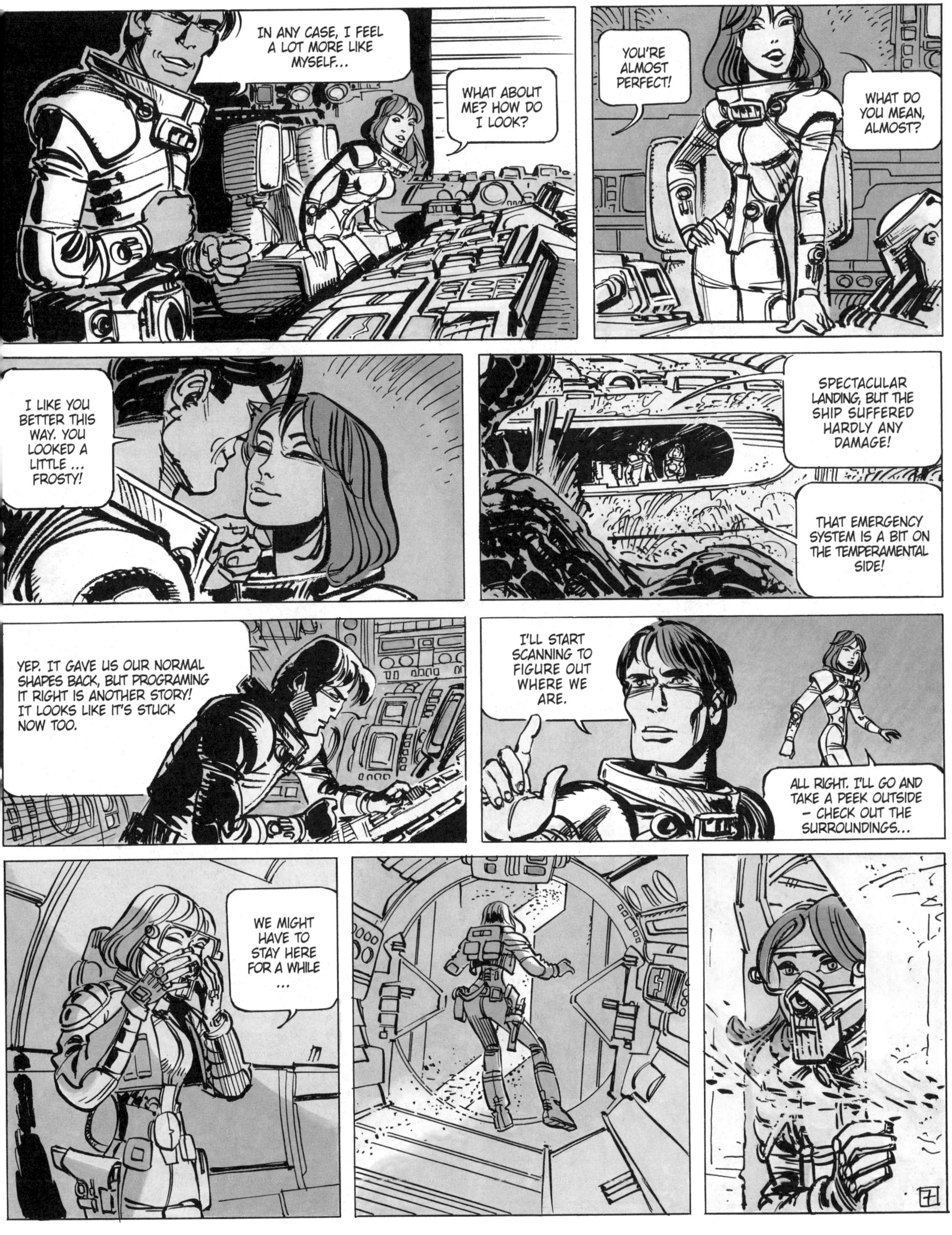
IN ANY CASE, I FEEL A LOT MORE LIKE MYSELF...
WHAT ABOUT ME? HOW DO I LOOK?
YOU'RE ALMOST PERFECT!
WHAT DO YOU MEAN, ALMOST?
I LIKE YOU BETTER THIS WAY. YOU LOOKED A LITTLE ... FROSTY!
SPECTACULAR LANDING, BUT THE SHIP SUFFERED HARDLY ANY DAMAGE!
THAT EMERGENCY SYSTEM IS A BIT ON THE TEMPERAMENTAL SIDE!
YEP. IT GAVE US OUR NORMAL SHAPES BACK, BUT PROGRAMING IT RIGHT IS ANOTHER STORY! IT LOOKS LIKE IT'S STUCK NOW TOO.
I'LL START SCANNING TO FIGURE OUT WHERE WE ARE.
ALL RIGHT. I'LL GO AND TAKE A PEEK OUTSIDE – CHECK OUT THE SURROUNDINGS...
WE MIGHT HAVE TO STAY HERE FOR A WHILE ...
7

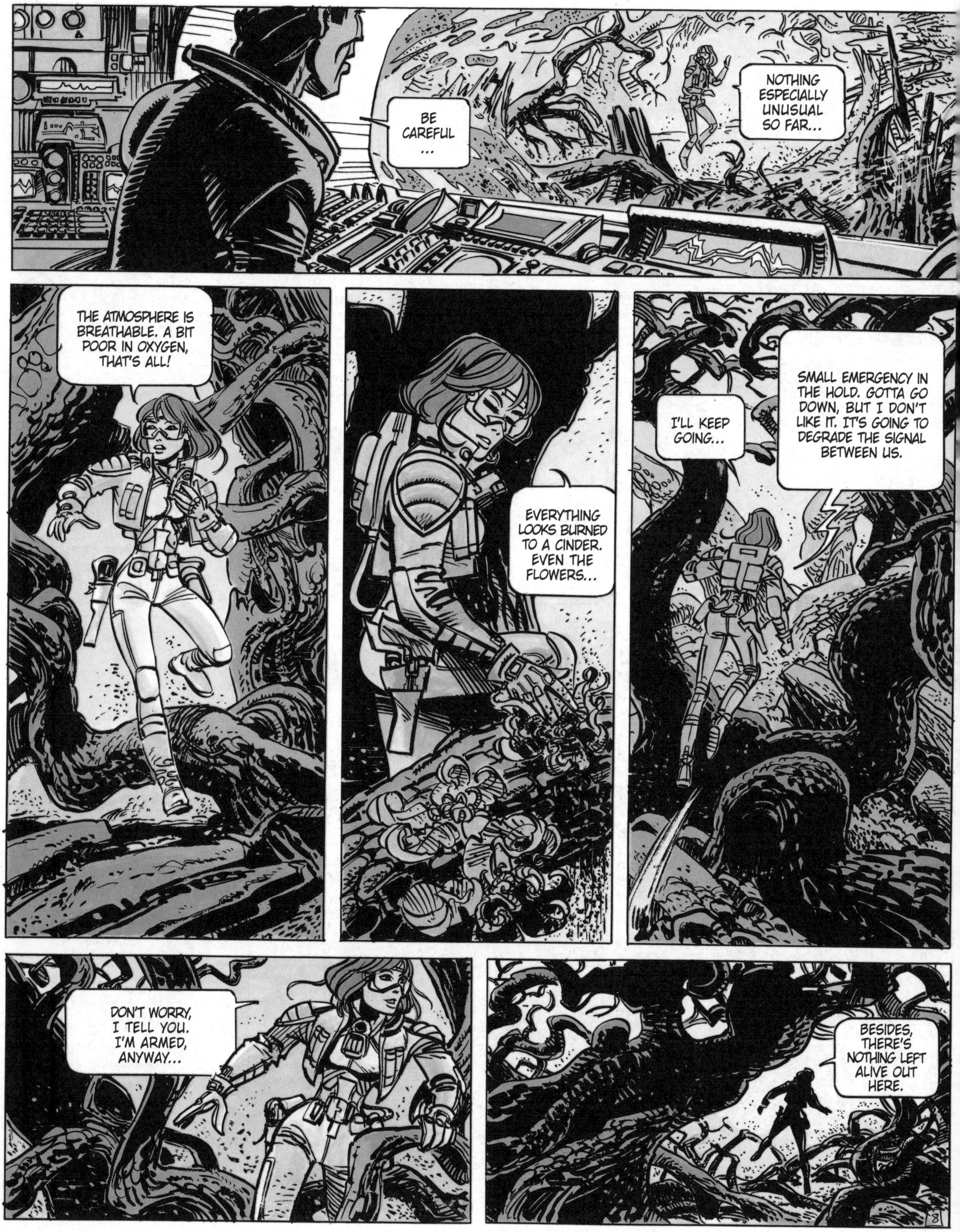
BE CAREFUL ...
NOTHING ESPECIALLY UNUSUAL SO FAR...
THE ATMOSPHERE IS BREATHABLE. A BIT POOR IN OXYGEN, THAT'S ALL!
EVERYTHING LOOKS BURNED TO A CINDER. EVEN THE FLOWERS...
SMALL EMERGENCY IN THE HOLD. GOTTA GO DOWN, BUT I DON'T LIKE IT. IT'S GOING TO DEGRADE THE SIGNAL BETWEEN US.
I'LL KEEP GOING...
DON'T WORRY, I TELL YOU. I'M ARMED, ANYWAY...
BESIDES, THERE'S NOTHING LEFT ALIVE OUT HERE.

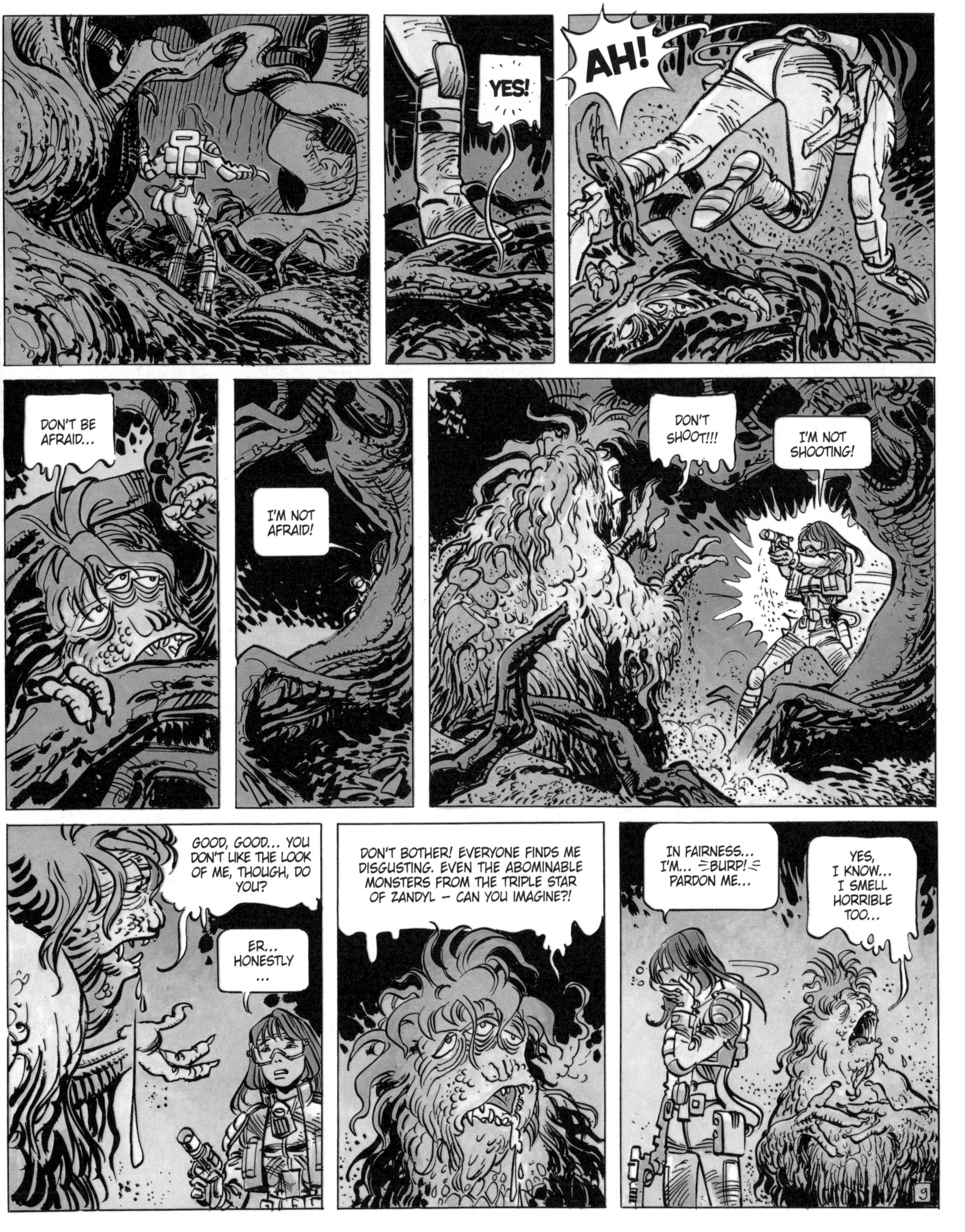

YES!
AH!
DON'T BE AFRAID...
I'M NOT AFRAID!
DON'T SHOOT!!!
I'M NOT SHOOTING!
GOOD, GOOD... YOU DON'T LIKE THE LOOK OF ME, THOUGH, DO YOU?
ER... HONESTLY ...
DON'T BOTHER! EVERYONE FINDS ME DISGUSTING. EVEN THE ABOMINABLE MONSTERS FROM THE TRIPLE STAR OF ZANDYL – CAN YOU IMAGINE?!
IN FAIRNESS... I'M... BURP! PARDON ME...
YES, I KNOW... I SMELL HORRIBLE TOO...
9

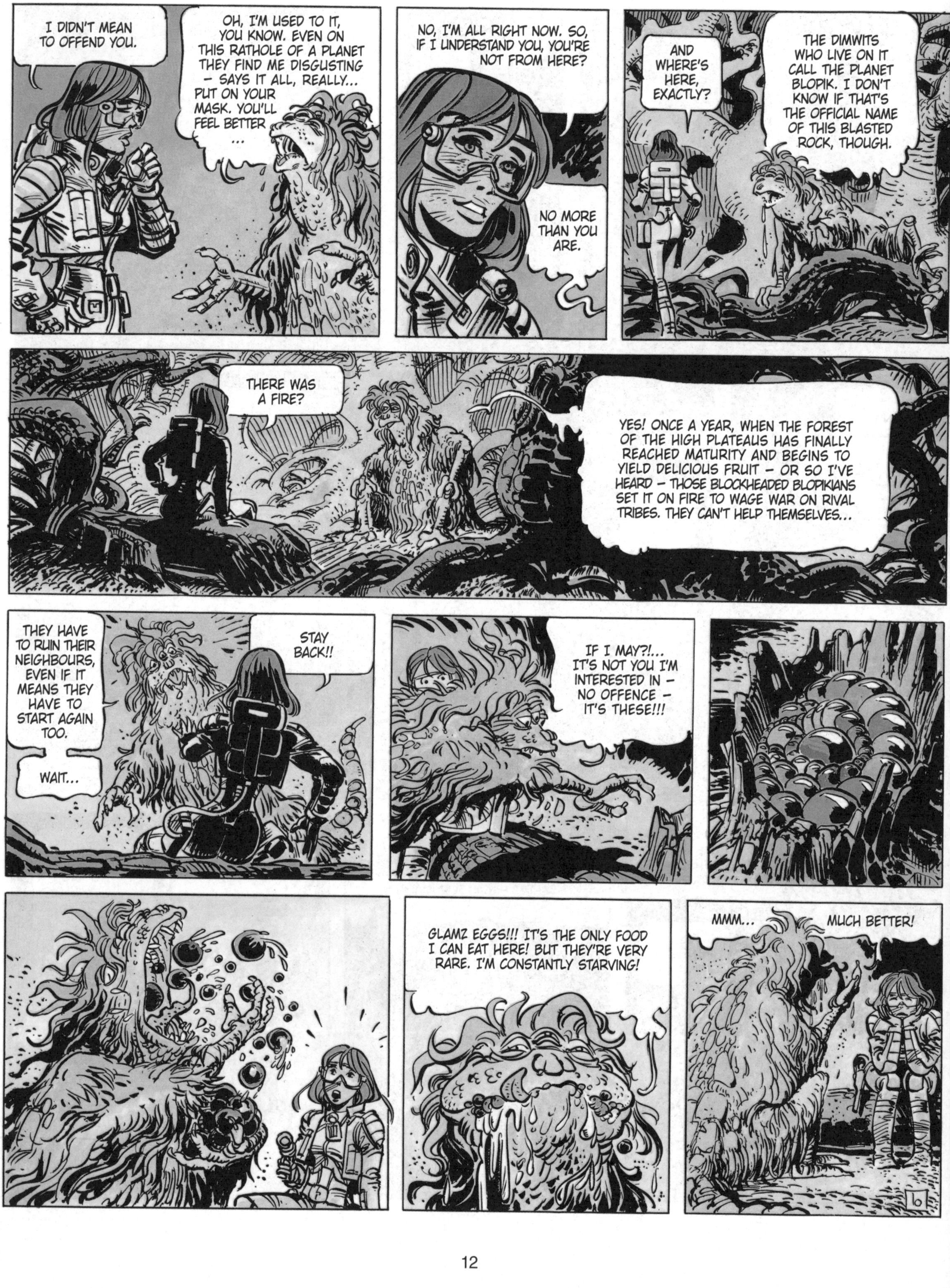
I DIDN'T MEAN TO OFFEND YOU.
OH, I'M USED TO IT, YOU KNOW. EVEN ON THIS RATHOLE OF A PLANET THEY FIND ME DISGUSTING – SAYS IT ALL, REALLY... PUT ON YOUR MASK. YOU'LL FEEL BETTER ...
NO, I'M ALL RIGHT NOW. SO, IF I UNDERSTAND YOU, YOU'RE NOT FROM HERE?
NO MORE THAN YOU ARE.
AND WHERE'S HERE, EXACTLY?
THE DIMWITS WHO LIVE ON IT CALL THE PLANET BLOPIK. I DON'T KNOW IF THAT'S THE OFFICIAL NAME OF THIS BLASTED ROCK, THOUGH.
THERE WAS A FIRE?
YES! ONCE A YEAR, WHEN THE FOREST OF THE HIGH PLATEAUS HAS FINALLY REACHED MATURITY AND BEGINS TO YIELD DELICIOUS FRUIT – OR SO I'VE HEARD – THOSE BLOCKHEADED BLOPIKIANS SET IT ON FIRE TO WAGE WAR ON RIVAL TRIBES. THEY CAN'T HELP THEMSELVES...
THEY HAVE TO RUIN THEIR NEIGHBOURS, EVEN IF IT MEANS THEY HAVE TO START AGAIN TOO.
WAIT...
STAY BACK!!
IF I MAY?!... IT'S NOT YOU I'M INTERESTED IN – NO OFFENCE – IT'S THESE!!!
GLAMZ EGGS!!! IT'S THE ONLY FOOD I CAN EAT HERE! BUT THEY'RE VERY RARE. I'M CONSTANTLY STARVING!
MMM...
MUCH BETTER!

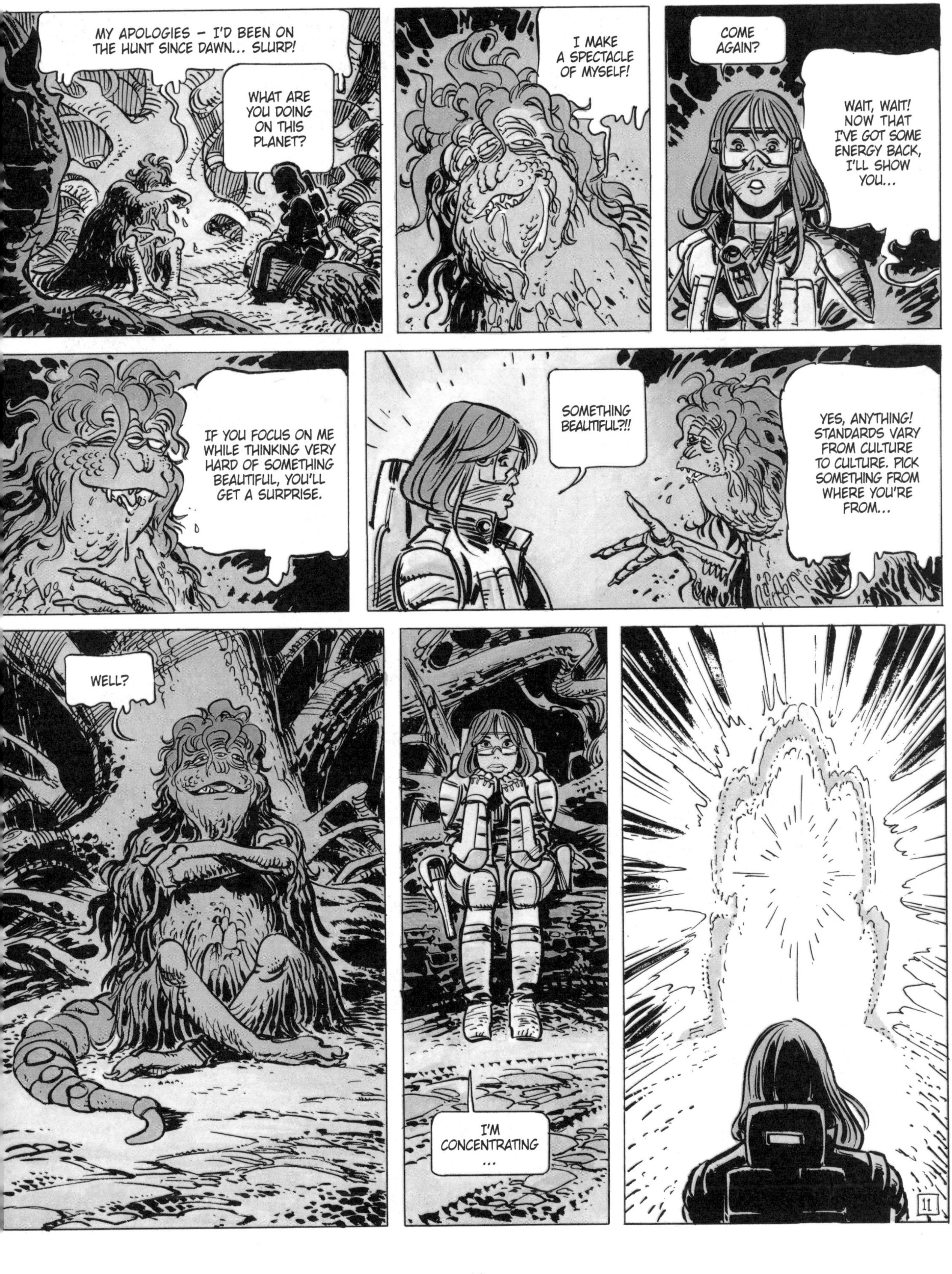
MY APOLOGIES – I'D BEEN ON THE HUNT SINCE DAWN... SLURP!
WHAT ARE YOU DOING ON THIS PLANET?
I MAKE A SPECTACLE OF MYSELF!
COME AGAIN?
WAIT, WAIT! NOW THAT I'VE GOT SOME ENERGY BACK, I'LL SHOW YOU...
IF YOU FOCUS ON ME WHILE THINKING VERY HARD OF SOMETHING BEAUTIFUL, YOU'LL GET A SURPRISE.
SOMETHING BEAUTIFUL?!!
YES, ANYTHING! STANDARDS VARY FROM CULTURE TO CULTURE. PICK SOMETHING FROM WHERE YOU'RE FROM...
WELL?
I'M CONCENTRATING ...
11

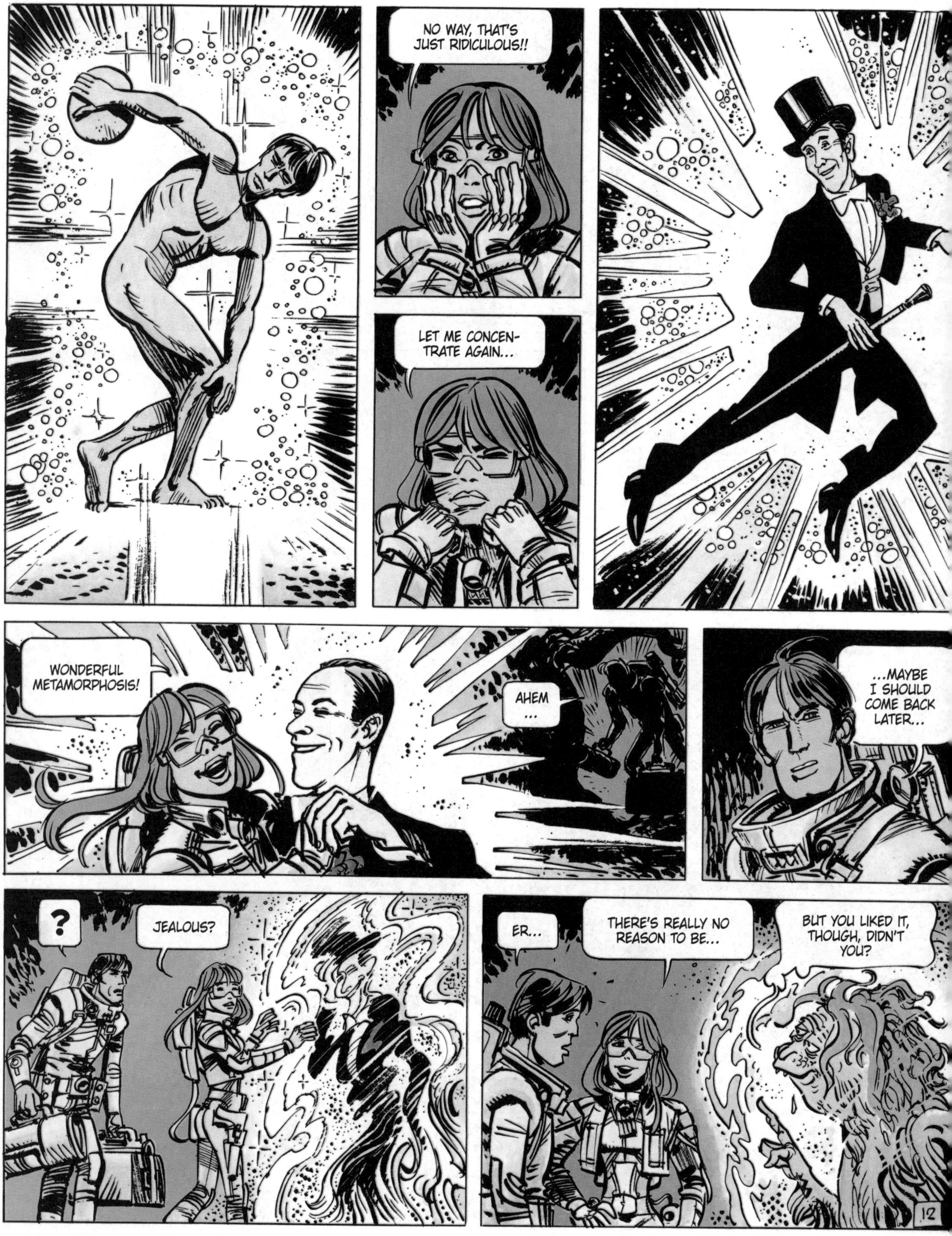
NO WAY, THAT'S JUST RIDICULOUS!!
LET ME CONCEN-TRATE AGAIN...
WONDERFUL METAMORPHOSIS!
AHEM ...
...MAYBE I SHOULD COME BACK LATER...
?
JEALOUS?
ER...
THERE'S REALLY NO REASON TO BE...
BUT YOU LIKED IT, THOUGH, DIDN'T YOU?
12

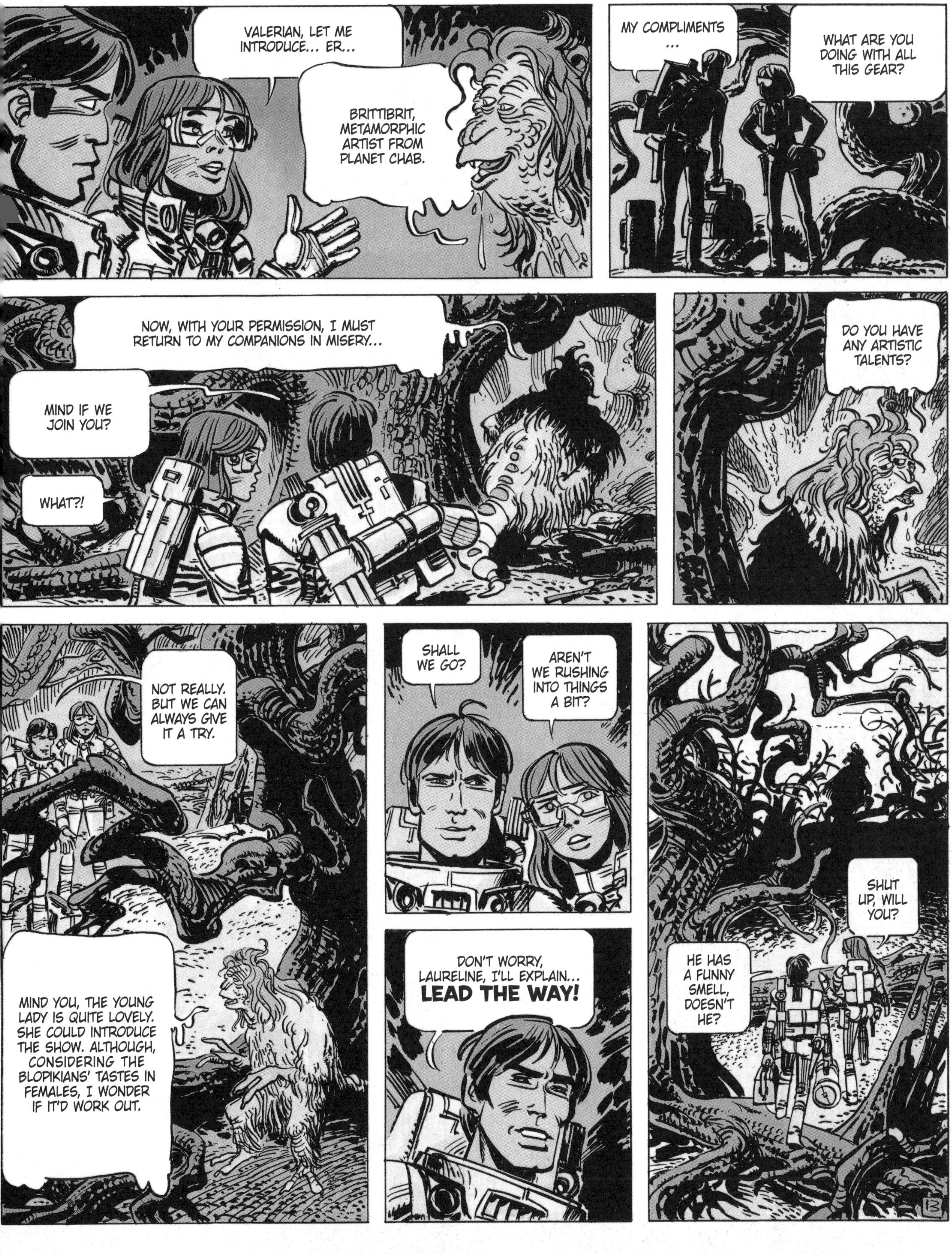
VALERIAN, LET ME INTRODUCE... ER...
BRITTIBRIT, METAMORPHIC ARTIST FROM PLANET CHAB.
MY COMPLIMENTS ...
WHAT ARE YOU DOING WITH ALL THIS GEAR?
NOW, WITH YOUR PERMISSION, I MUST RETURN TO MY COMPANIONS IN MISERY...
MIND IF WE JOIN YOU?
WHAT?!
DO YOU HAVE ANY ARTISTIC TALENTS?
NOT REALLY. BUT WE CAN ALWAYS GIVE IT A TRY.
MIND YOU, THE YOUNG LADY IS QUITE LOVELY. SHE COULD INTRODUCE THE SHOW. ALTHOUGH, CONSIDERING THE BLOPIKIANS' TASTES IN FEMALES, I WONDER IF IT'D WORK OUT.
SHALL WE GO?
AREN'T WE RUSHING INTO THINGS A BIT?
DON'T WORRY, LAURELINE, I'LL EXPLAIN... **LEAD THE WAY!**
HE HAS A FUNNY SMELL, DOESN'T HE?
SHUT UP, WILL YOU?

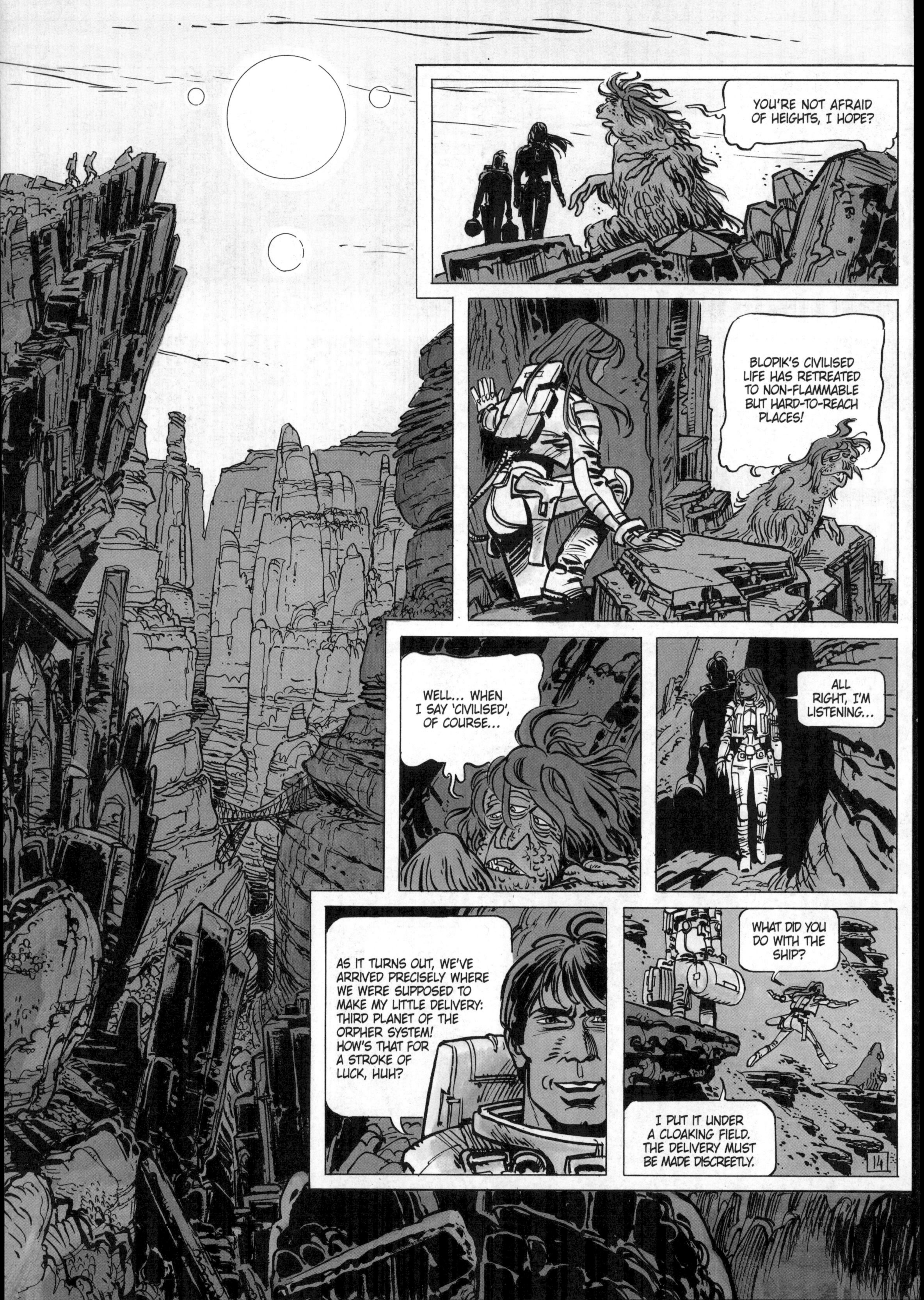
YOU'RE NOT AFRAID OF HEIGHTS, I HOPE?
BLOPIK'S CIVILISED LIFE HAS RETREATED TO NON-FLAMMABLE BUT HARD-TO-REACH PLACES!
WELL... WHEN I SAY 'CIVILISED', OF COURSE...
ALL RIGHT, I'M LISTENING...
AS IT TURNS OUT, WE'VE ARRIVED PRECISELY WHERE WE WERE SUPPOSED TO MAKE MY LITTLE DELIVERY: THIRD PLANET OF THE ORPHER SYSTEM! HOW'S THAT FOR A STROKE OF LUCK, HUH?
WHAT DID YOU DO WITH THE SHIP?
I PUT IT UNDER A CLOAKING FIELD. THE DELIVERY MUST BE MADE DISCREETLY.
14

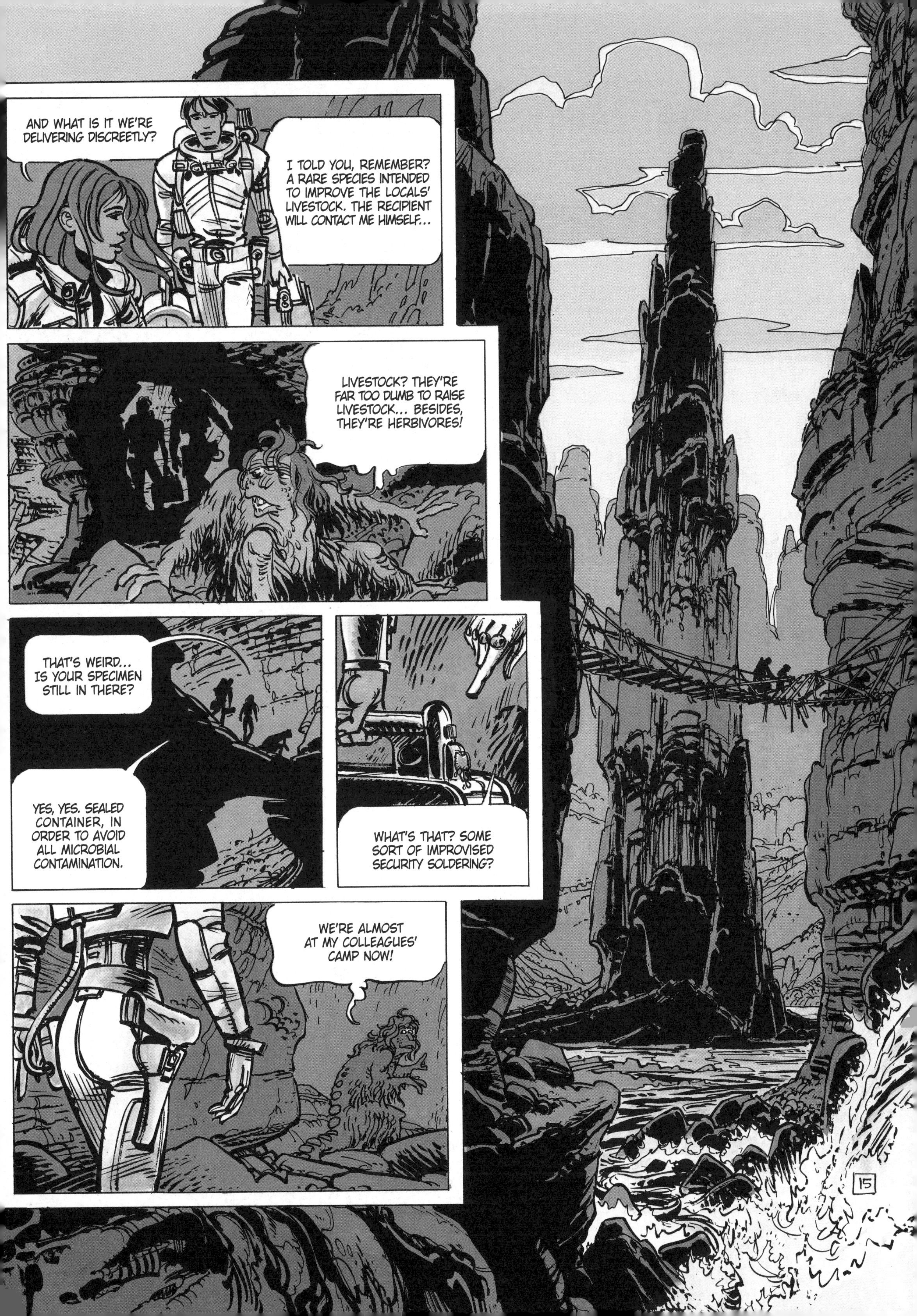
AND WHAT IS IT WE'RE DELIVERING DISCREETLY?
I TOLD YOU, REMEMBER? A RARE SPECIES INTENDED TO IMPROVE THE LOCALS' LIVESTOCK. THE RECIPIENT WILL CONTACT ME HIMSELF...
LIVESTOCK? THEY'RE FAR TOO DUMB TO RAISE LIVESTOCK... BESIDES, THEY'RE HERBIVORES!
THAT'S WEIRD... IS YOUR SPECIMEN STILL IN THERE?
YES, YES. SEALED CONTAINER, IN ORDER TO AVOID ALL MICROBIAL CONTAMINATION.
WHAT'S THAT? SOME SORT OF IMPROVISED SECURITY SOLDERING?
WE'RE ALMOST AT MY COLLEAGUES' CAMP NOW!
15

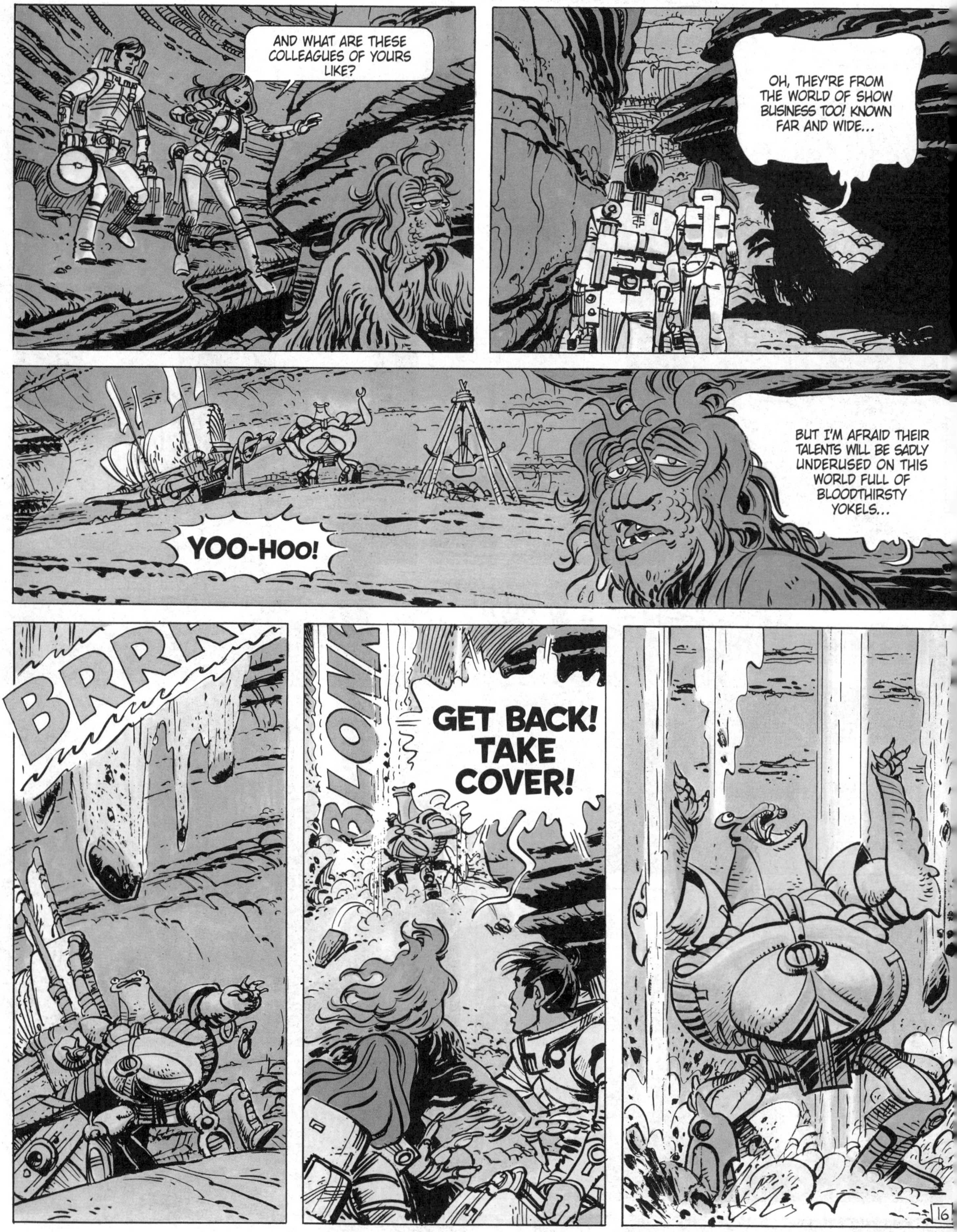
AND WHAT ARE THESE COLLEAGUES OF YOURS LIKE?
OH, THEY'RE FROM THE WORLD OF SHOW BUSINESS TOO! KNOWN FAR AND WIDE...
BUT I'M AFRAID THEIR TALENTS WILL BE SADLY UNDERUSED ON THIS WORLD FULL OF BLOODTHIRSTY YOKELS...
YOO-HOO!
BRRR
BLONK
GET BACK! TAKE COVER!
16

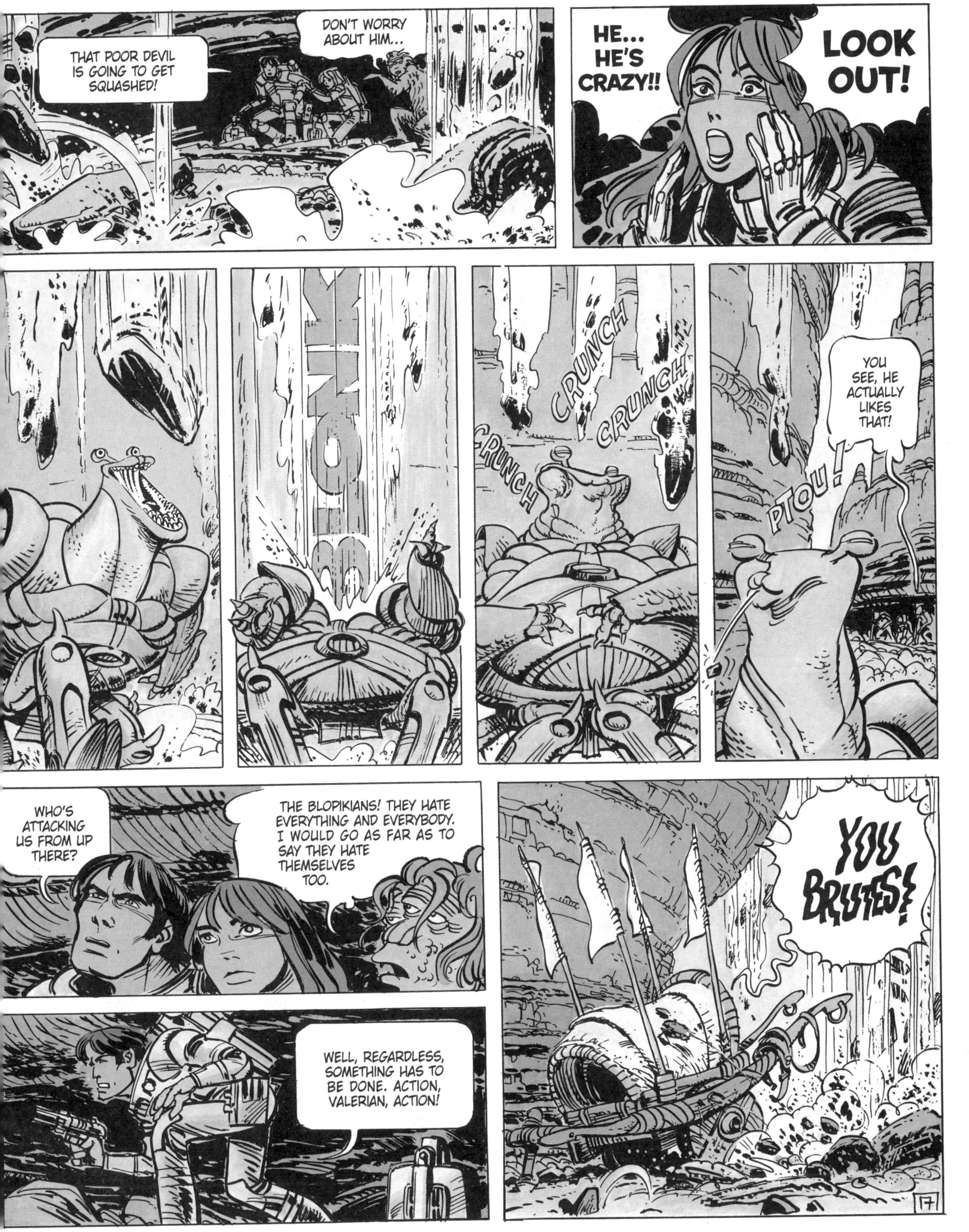
THAT POOR DEVIL IS GOING TO GET SQUASHED!
DON'T WORRY ABOUT HIM...
HE... HE'S CRAZY!!
LOOK OUT!
CRUNCH
CRUNCH
CRUNCH
YOU SEE, HE ACTUALLY LIKES THAT!
PTOU!
WHO'S ATTACKING US FROM UP THERE?
THE BLOPIKIANS! THEY HATE EVERYTHING AND EVERYBODY. I WOULD GO AS FAR AS TO SAY THEY HATE THEMSELVES TOO.
YOU BRUTES!
WELL, REGARDLESS, SOMETHING HAS TO BE DONE. ACTION, VALERIAN, ACTION!
17

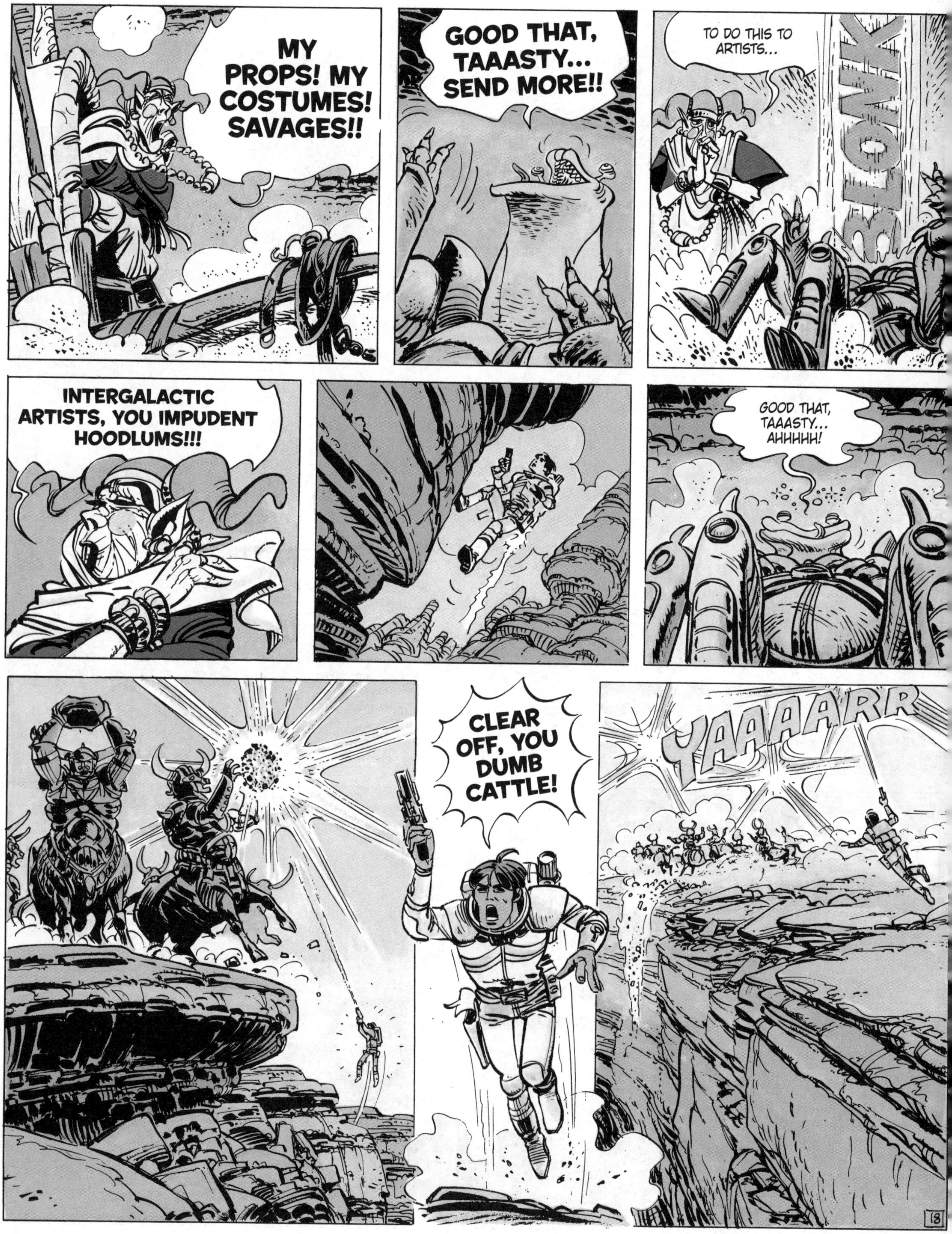

MY PROPS! MY COSTUMES! SAVAGES!!
GOOD THAT, TAAASTY... SEND MORE!!
TO DO THIS TO ARTISTS...
BLONK
INTERGALACTIC ARTISTS, YOU IMPUDENT HOODLUMS!!!
GOOD THAT, TAAASTY... AHHHHH!
CLEAR OFF, YOU DUMB CATTLE!
YAAAAARR
18

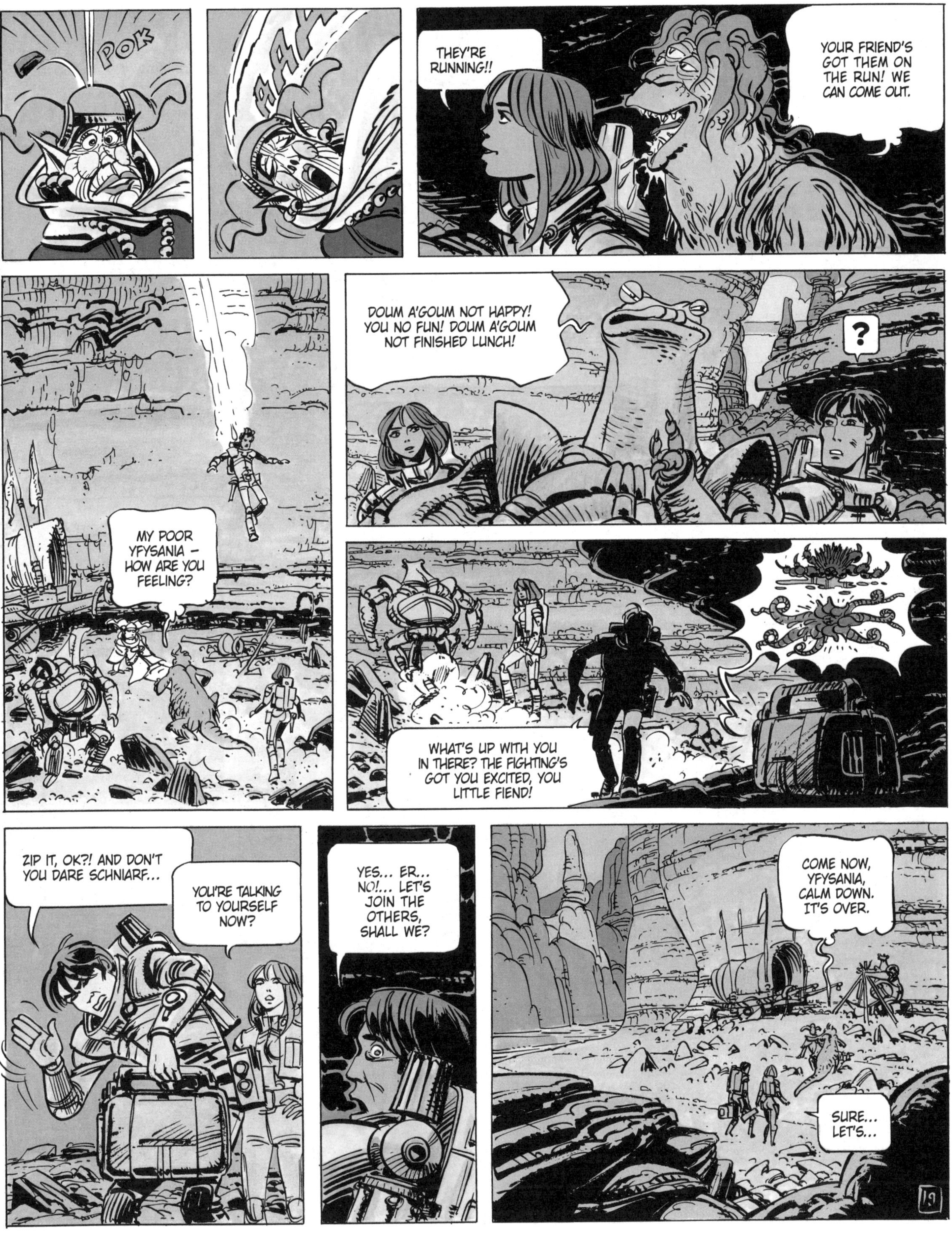
POK
THEY'RE RUNNING!!
YOUR FRIEND'S GOT THEM ON THE RUN! WE CAN COME OUT.
MY POOR YFYSANIA – HOW ARE YOU FEELING?
DOUM A'GOUM NOT HAPPY! YOU NO FUN! DOUM A'GOUM NOT FINISHED LUNCH!
?
WHAT'S UP WITH YOU IN THERE? THE FIGHTING'S GOT YOU EXCITED, YOU LITTLE FIEND!
ZIP IT, OK?! AND DON'T YOU DARE SCHNIARF...
YOU'RE TALKING TO YOURSELF NOW?
YES... ER... NO!... LET'S JOIN THE OTHERS, SHALL WE?
COME NOW, YFYSANIA, CALM DOWN. IT'S OVER.
SURE... LET'S...
19

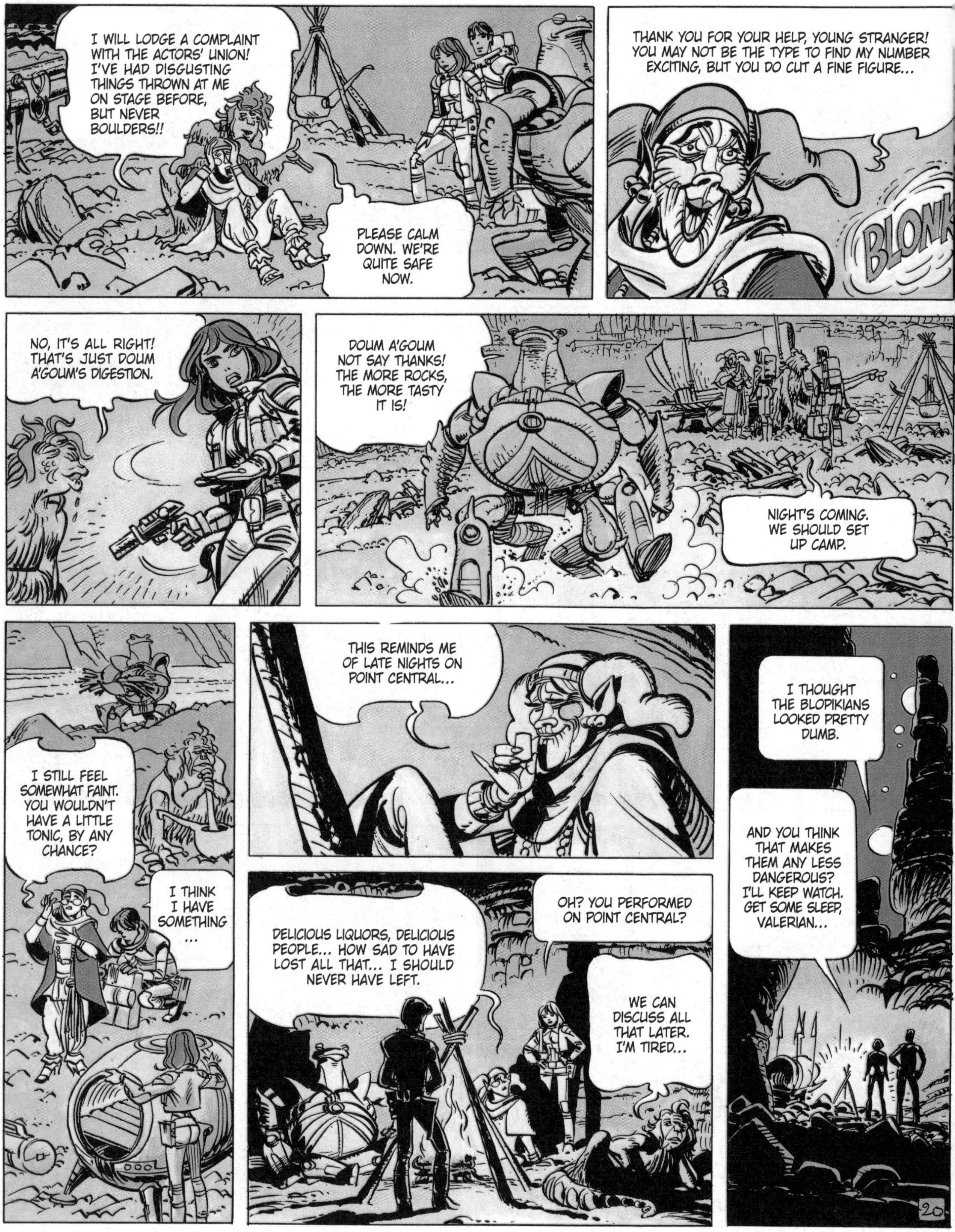
I WILL LODGE A COMPLAINT WITH THE ACTORS' UNION! I'VE HAD DISGUSTING THINGS THROWN AT ME ON STAGE BEFORE, BUT NEVER BOULDERS!!
PLEASE CALM DOWN. WE'RE QUITE SAFE NOW.
THANK YOU FOR YOUR HELP, YOUNG STRANGER! YOU MAY NOT BE THE TYPE TO FIND MY NUMBER EXCITING, BUT YOU DO CUT A FINE FIGURE...
BLONK
NO, IT'S ALL RIGHT! THAT'S JUST DOUM A'GOUM'S DIGESTION.
DOUM A'GOUM NOT SAY THANKS! THE MORE ROCKS, THE MORE TASTY IT IS!
NIGHT'S COMING. WE SHOULD SET UP CAMP.
I STILL FEEL SOMEWHAT FAINT. YOU WOULDN'T HAVE A LITTLE TONIC, BY ANY CHANCE?
I THINK I HAVE SOMETHING ...
THIS REMINDS ME OF LATE NIGHTS ON POINT CENTRAL...
DELICIOUS LIQUORS, DELICIOUS PEOPLE... HOW SAD TO HAVE LOST ALL THAT... I SHOULD NEVER HAVE LEFT.
OH? YOU PERFORMED ON POINT CENTRAL?
WE CAN DISCUSS ALL THAT LATER. I'M TIRED...
I THOUGHT THE BLOPIKIANS LOOKED PRETTY DUMB.
AND YOU THINK THAT MAKES THEM ANY LESS DANGEROUS? I'LL KEEP WATCH. GET SOME SLEEP, VALERIAN...
20

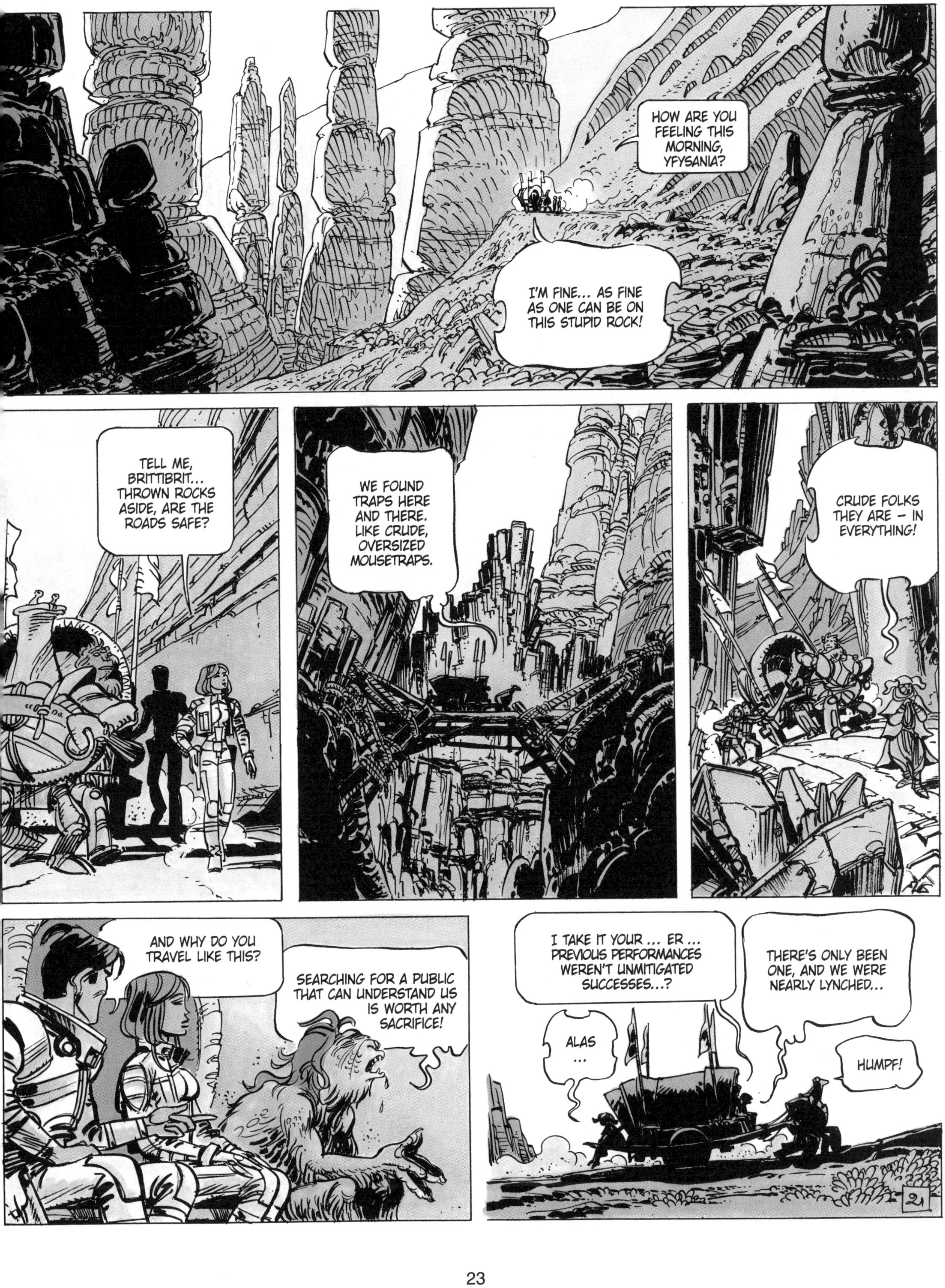
HOW ARE YOU FEELING THIS MORNING, YFYSANIA?
I'M FINE... AS FINE AS ONE CAN BE ON THIS STUPID ROCK!
TELL ME, BRITTIBRIT... THROWN ROCKS ASIDE, ARE THE ROADS SAFE?
WE FOUND TRAPS HERE AND THERE. LIKE CRUDE, OVERSIZED MOUSETRAPS.
CRUDE FOLKS THEY ARE – IN EVERYTHING!
AND WHY DO YOU TRAVEL LIKE THIS?
SEARCHING FOR A PUBLIC THAT CAN UNDERSTAND US IS WORTH ANY SACRIFICE!
I TAKE IT YOUR ... ER ... PREVIOUS PERFORMANCES WEREN'T UNMITIGATED SUCCESSES...?
ALAS ...
THERE'S ONLY BEEN ONE, AND WE WERE NEARLY LYNCHED...
HUMPF!
21

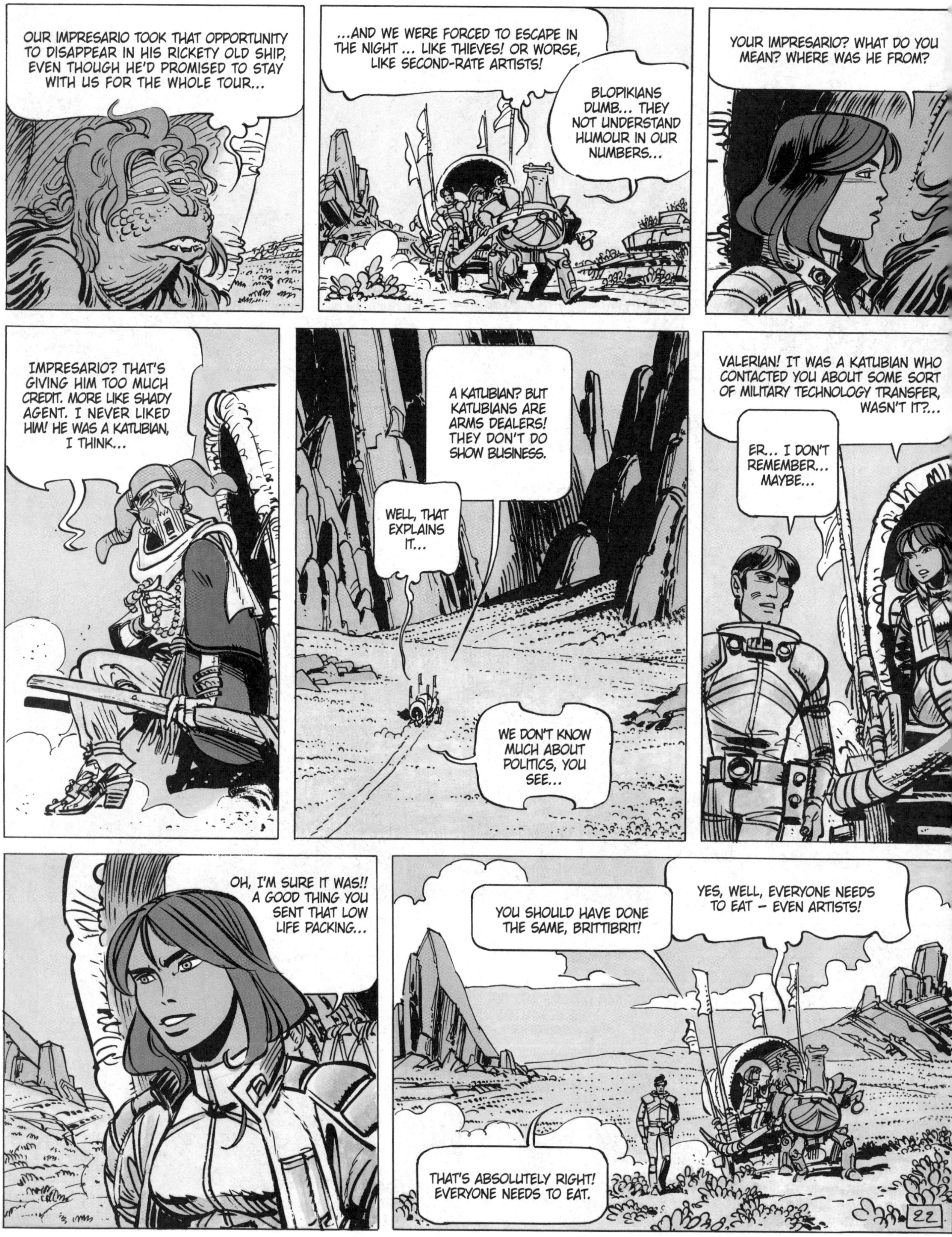

OUR IMPRESARIO TOOK THAT OPPORTUNITY TO DISAPPEAR IN HIS RICKETY OLD SHIP, EVEN THOUGH HE'D PROMISED TO STAY WITH US FOR THE WHOLE TOUR...
...AND WE WERE FORCED TO ESCAPE IN THE NIGHT ... LIKE THIEVES! OR WORSE, LIKE SECOND-RATE ARTISTS!
BLOPIKIANS DUMB... THEY NOT UNDERSTAND HUMOUR IN OUR NUMBERS...
YOUR IMPRESARIO? WHAT DO YOU MEAN? WHERE WAS HE FROM?
IMPRESARIO? THAT'S GIVING HIM TOO MUCH CREDIT. MORE LIKE SHADY AGENT. I NEVER LIKED HIM! HE WAS A KATUBIAN, I THINK...
A KATUBIAN? BUT KATUBIANS ARE ARMS DEALERS! THEY DON'T DO SHOW BUSINESS.
WELL, THAT EXPLAINS IT...
WE DON'T KNOW MUCH ABOUT POLITICS, YOU SEE...
VALERIAN! IT WAS A KATUBIAN WHO CONTACTED YOU ABOUT SOME SORT OF MILITARY TECHNOLOGY TRANSFER, WASN'T IT?...
ER... I DON'T REMEMBER... MAYBE...
OH, I'M SURE IT WAS!! A GOOD THING YOU SENT THAT LOW LIFE PACKING...
YOU SHOULD HAVE DONE THE SAME, BRITTIBRIT!
YES, WELL, EVERYONE NEEDS TO EAT – EVEN ARTISTS!
THAT'S ABSOLUTELY RIGHT! EVERYONE NEEDS TO EAT.
22

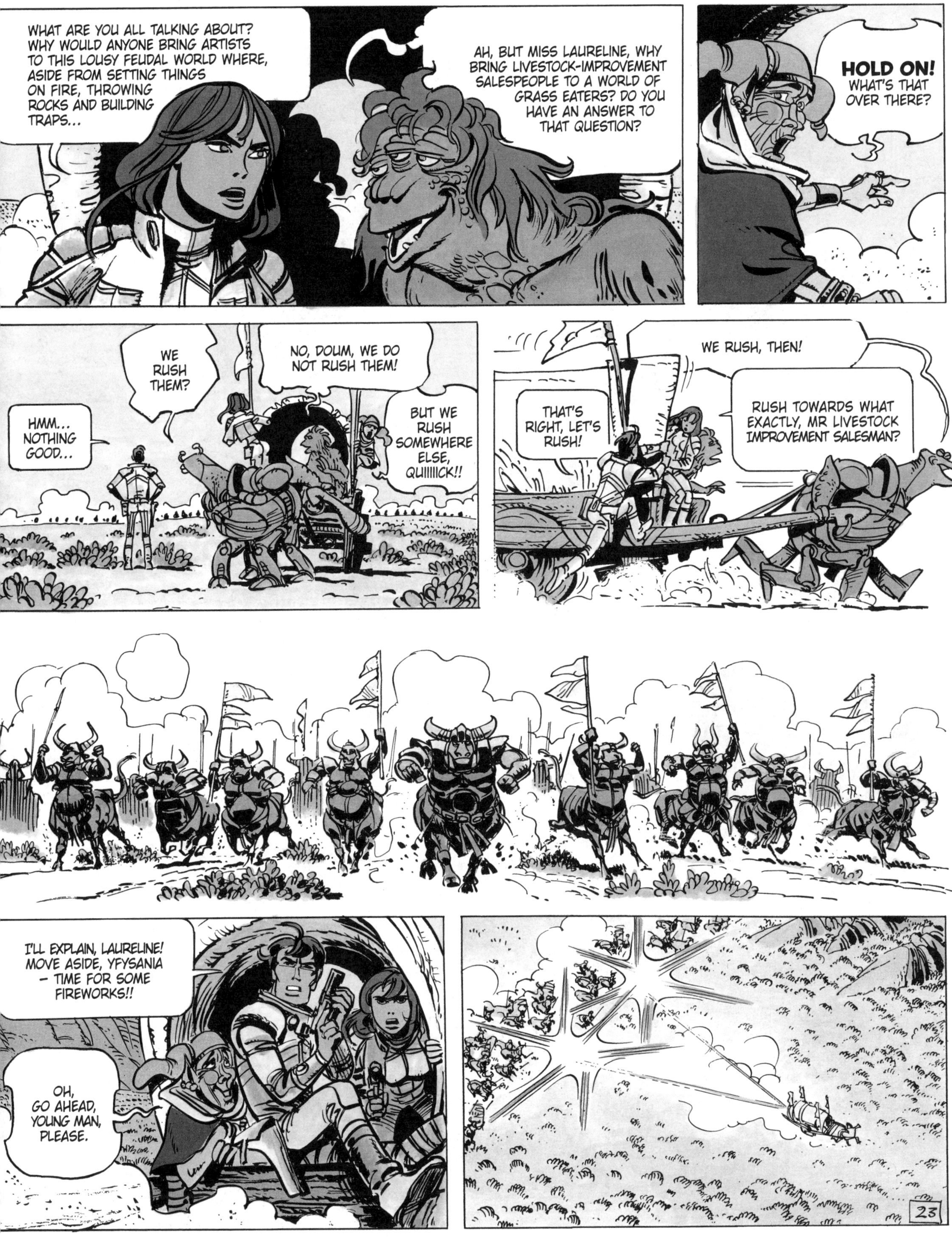
WHAT ARE YOU ALL TALKING ABOUT? WHY WOULD ANYONE BRING ARTISTS TO THIS LOUSY FEUDAL WORLD WHERE, ASIDE FROM SETTING THINGS ON FIRE, THROWING ROCKS AND BUILDING TRAPS...
AH, BUT MISS LAURELINE, WHY BRING LIVESTOCK-IMPROVEMENT SALESPEOPLE TO A WORLD OF GRASS EATERS? DO YOU HAVE AN ANSWER TO THAT QUESTION?
HOLD ON! WHAT'S THAT OVER THERE?
HMM... NOTHING GOOD...
WE RUSH THEM?
NO, DOUM, WE DO NOT RUSH THEM!
BUT WE RUSH SOMEWHERE ELSE, QUIIIIICK!!
WE RUSH, THEN!
THAT'S RIGHT, LET'S RUSH!
RUSH TOWARDS WHAT EXACTLY, MR LIVESTOCK IMPROVEMENT SALESMAN?
I'LL EXPLAIN, LAURELINE! MOVE ASIDE, YFYSANIA – TIME FOR SOME FIREWORKS!!
OH, GO AHEAD, YOUNG MAN, PLEASE.
23

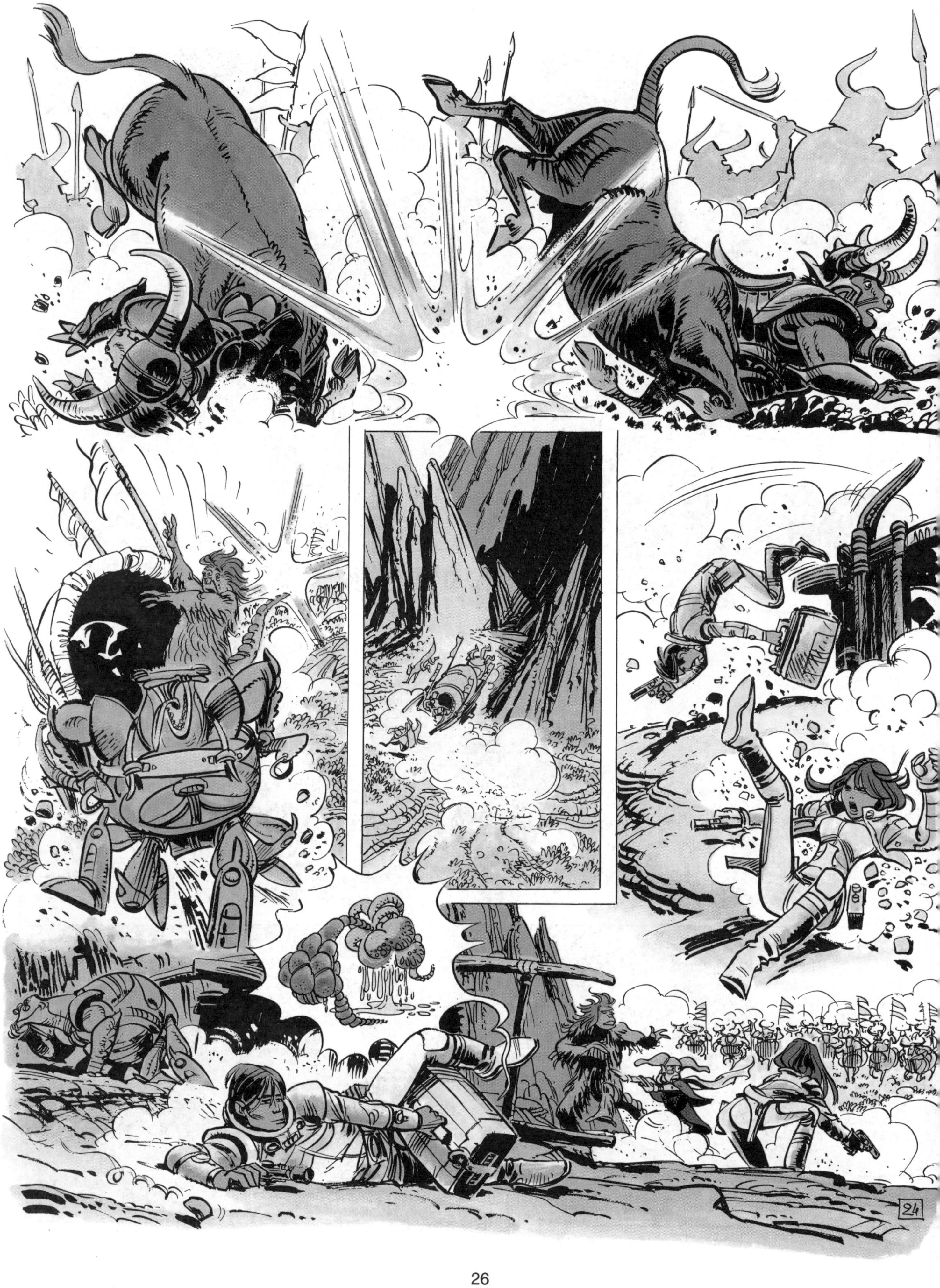

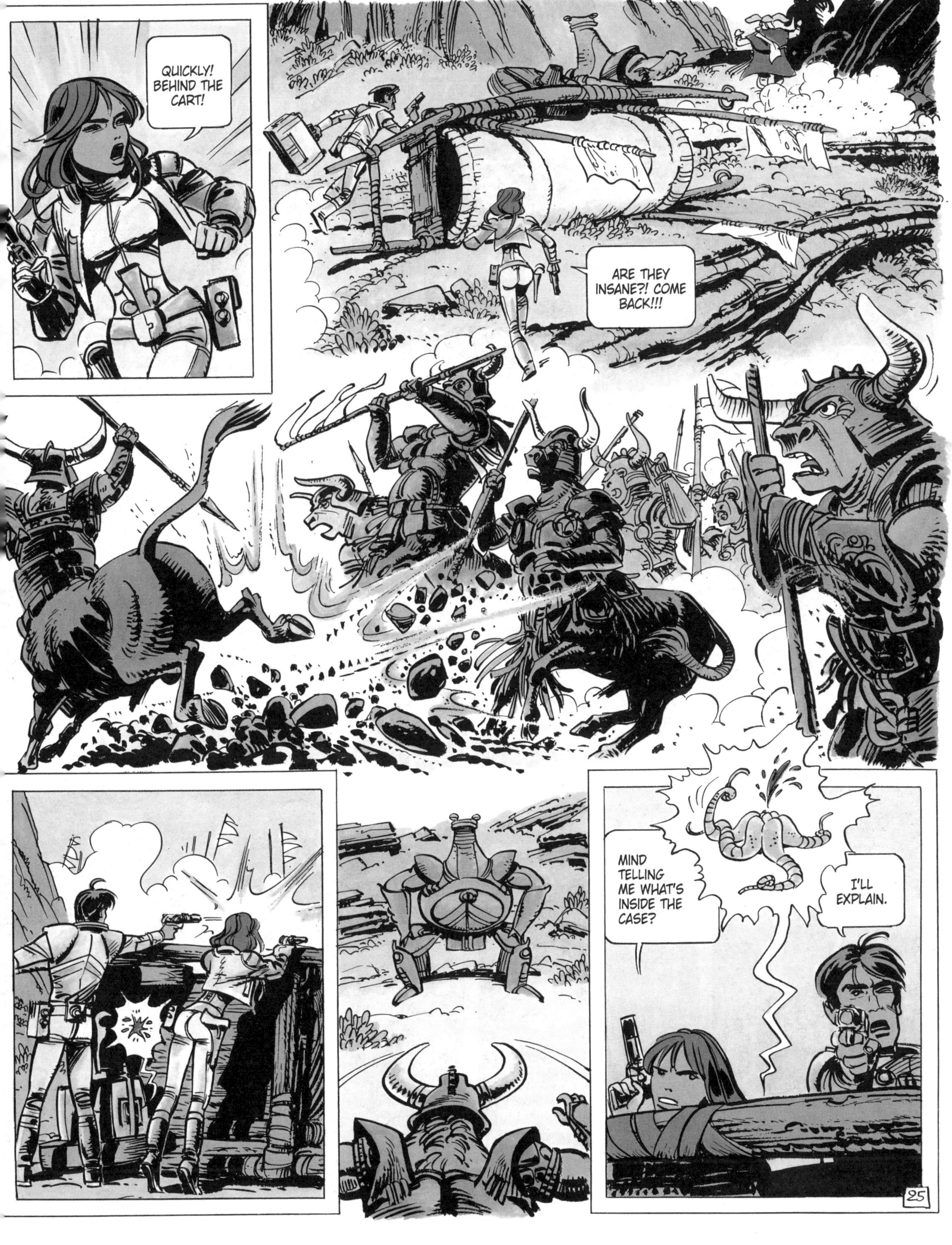
QUICKLY! BEHIND THE CART!
ARE THEY INSANE?! COME BACK!!!
MIND TELLING ME WHAT'S INSIDE THE CASE?
I'LL EXPLAIN.
25

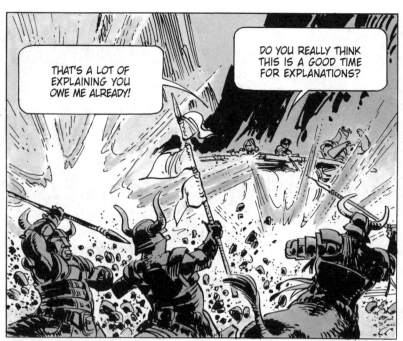

THAT'S A LOT OF EXPLAINING YOU OWE ME ALREADY!

DO YOU REALLY THINK THIS IS A GOOD TIME FOR EXPLANATIONS?

IT'S ALWAYS A GOOD TIME FOR EXPLANATIONS — EVEN IN THE MIDDLE OF ACTION!

COURSE IT IS...

TSHAK TSHAK TSHAK

EEEEEEEE

YFYSANIA'S VOICE!!

AAAA

OH DEAR! THIS TRAP WORKED JUST FINE!!

28

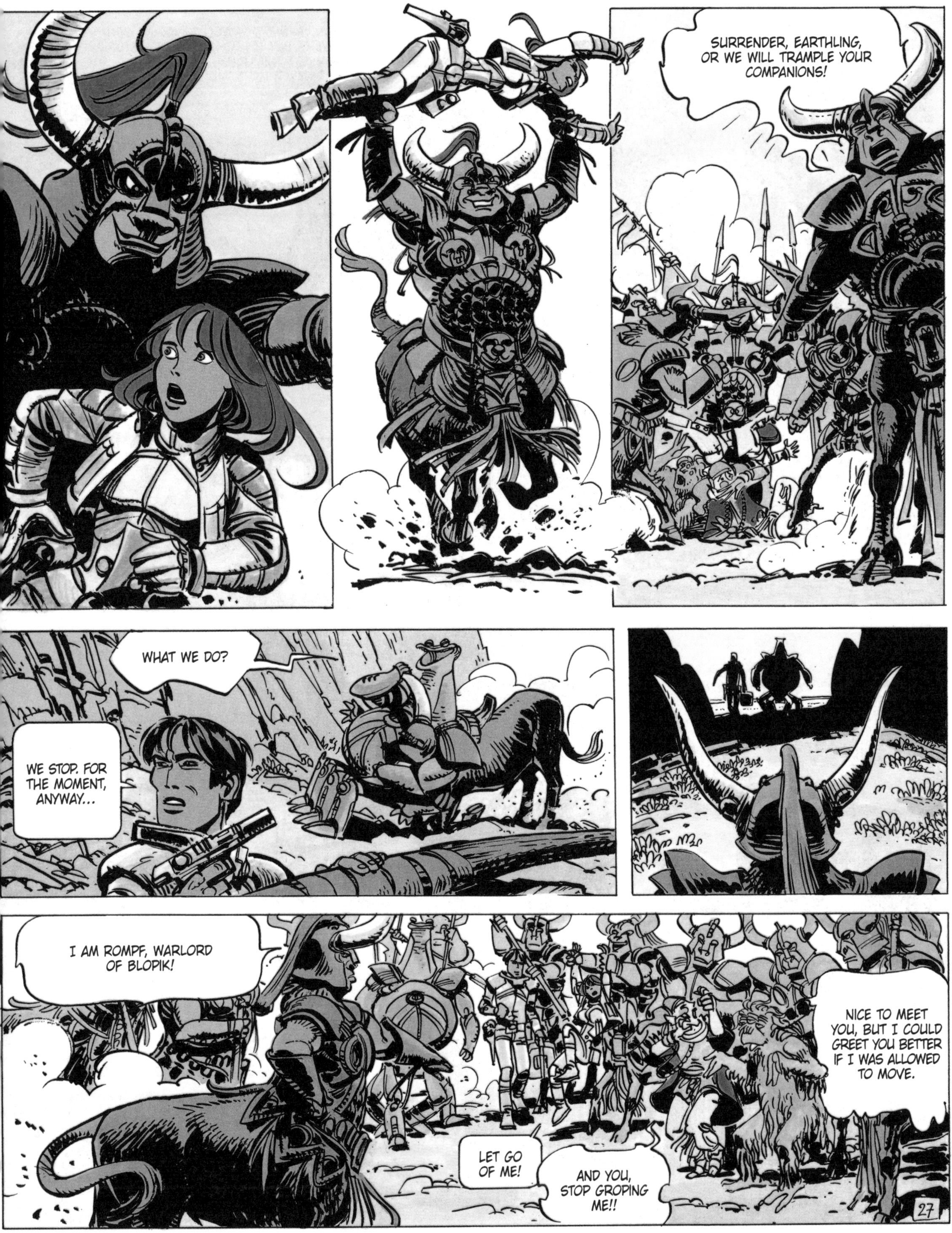
SURRENDER, EARTHLING, OR WE WILL TRAMPLE YOUR COMPANIONS!
WHAT WE DO?
WE STOP. FOR THE MOMENT, ANYWAY...
I AM ROMPF, WARLORD OF BLOPIK!
NICE TO MEET YOU, BUT I COULD GREET YOU BETTER IF I WAS ALLOWED TO MOVE.
LET GO OF ME!
AND YOU, STOP GROPING ME!!
27

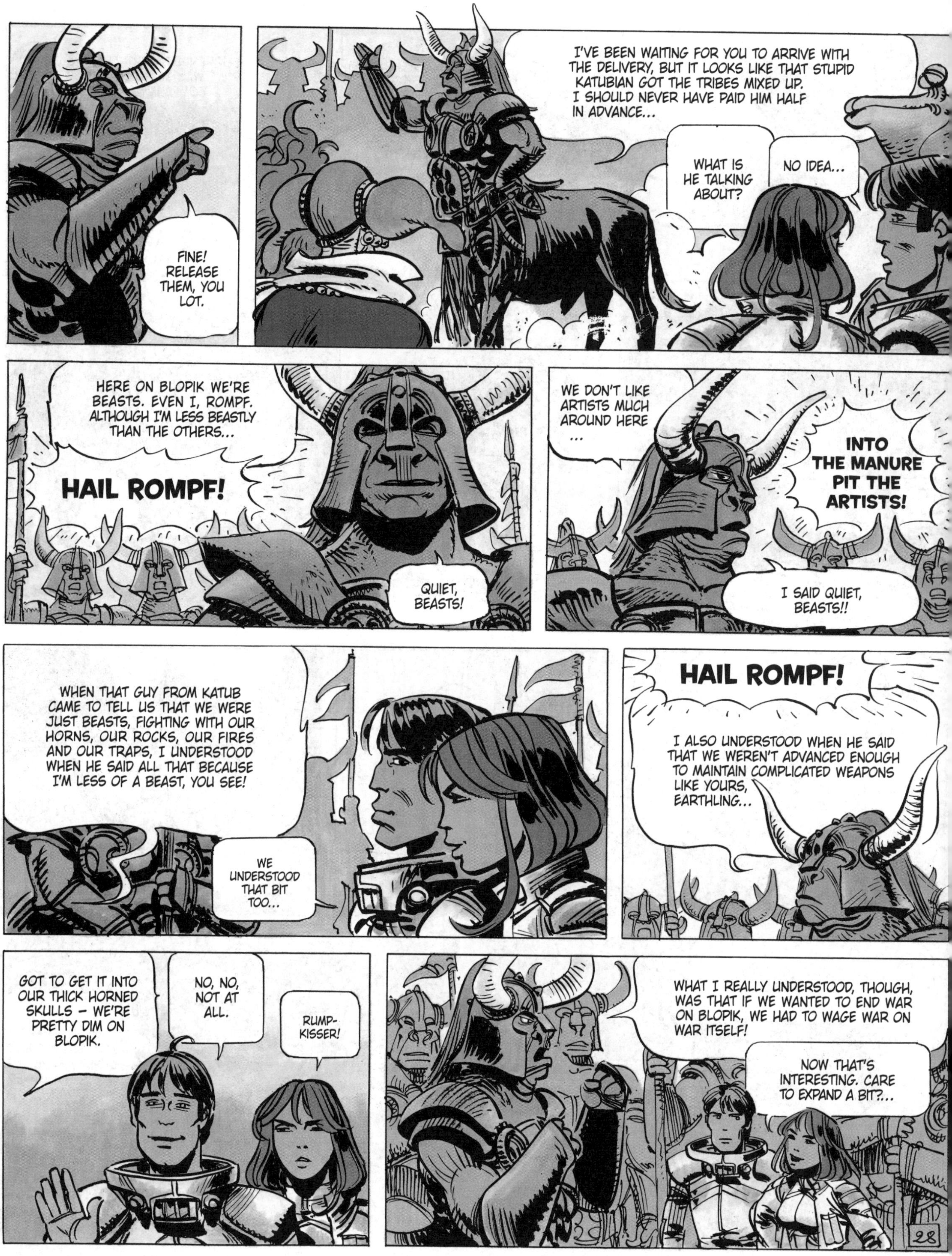
FINE! RELEASE THEM, YOU LOT.
I'VE BEEN WAITING FOR YOU TO ARRIVE WITH THE DELIVERY, BUT IT LOOKS LIKE THAT STUPID KATUBIAN GOT THE TRIBES MIXED UP. I SHOULD NEVER HAVE PAID HIM HALF IN ADVANCE...
WHAT IS HE TALKING ABOUT?
NO IDEA...
HERE ON BLOPIK WE'RE BEASTS. EVEN I, ROMPF. ALTHOUGH I'M LESS BEASTLY THAN THE OTHERS...
HAIL ROMPF!
QUIET, BEASTS!
WE DON'T LIKE ARTISTS MUCH AROUND HERE ...
INTO THE MANURE PIT THE ARTISTS!
I SAID QUIET, BEASTS!!
WHEN THAT GUY FROM KATUB CAME TO TELL US THAT WE WERE JUST BEASTS, FIGHTING WITH OUR HORNS, OUR ROCKS, OUR FIRES AND OUR TRAPS, I UNDERSTOOD WHEN HE SAID ALL THAT BECAUSE I'M LESS OF A BEAST, YOU SEE!
WE UNDERSTOOD THAT BIT TOO...
HAIL ROMPF!
I ALSO UNDERSTOOD WHEN HE SAID THAT WE WEREN'T ADVANCED ENOUGH TO MAINTAIN COMPLICATED WEAPONS LIKE YOURS, EARTHLING...
GOT TO GET IT INTO OUR THICK HORNED SKULLS – WE'RE PRETTY DIM ON BLOPIK.
NO, NO, NOT AT ALL.
RUMP-KISSER!
WHAT I REALLY UNDERSTOOD, THOUGH, WAS THAT IF WE WANTED TO END WAR ON BLOPIK, WE HAD TO WAGE WAR ON WAR ITSELF!
NOW THAT'S INTERESTING. CARE TO EXPAND A BIT?...
28

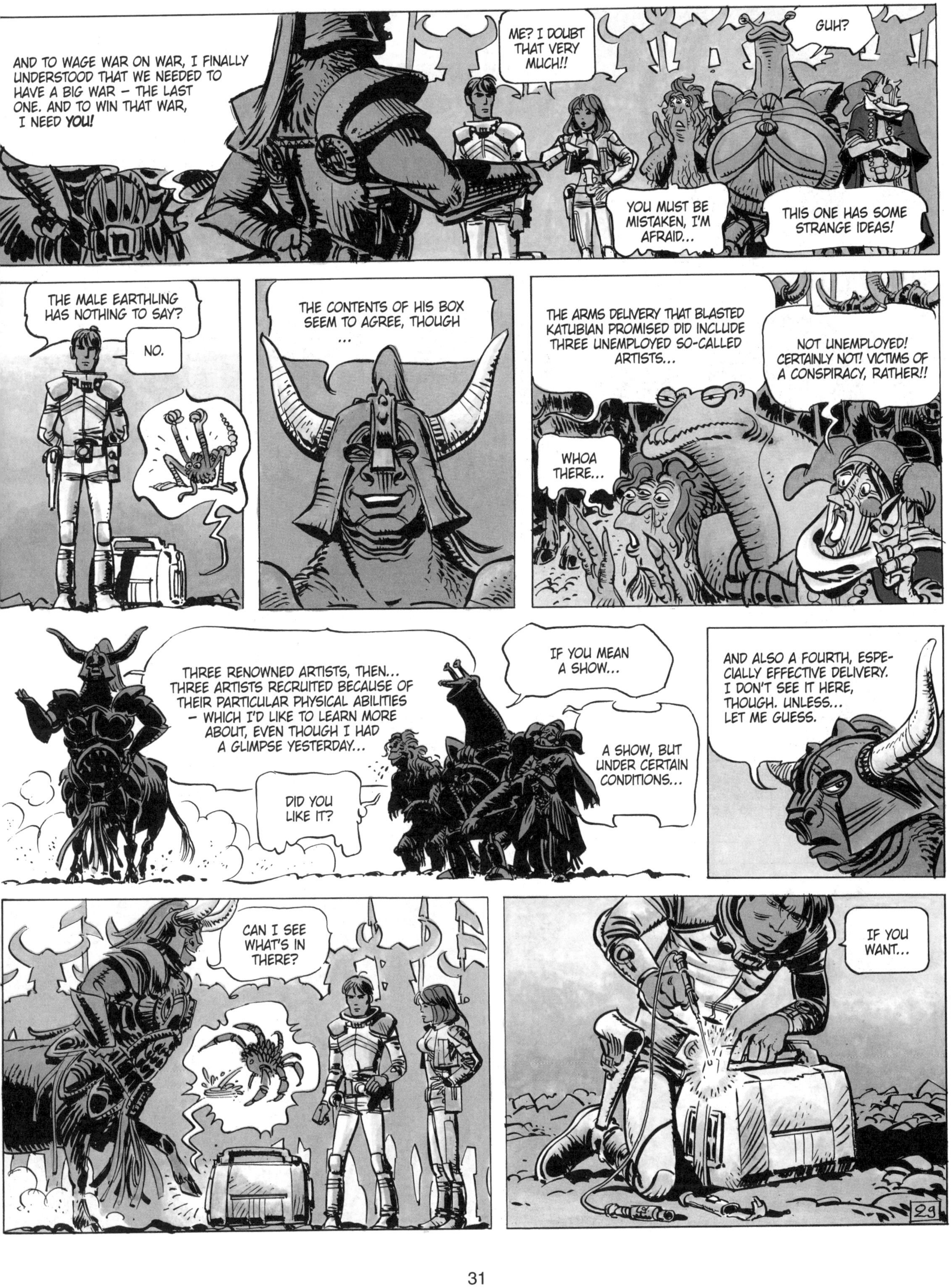
AND TO WAGE WAR ON WAR, I FINALLY UNDERSTOOD THAT WE NEEDED TO HAVE A BIG WAR – THE LAST ONE. AND TO WIN THAT WAR, I NEED YOU!
ME? I DOUBT THAT VERY MUCH!!
GUH?
YOU MUST BE MISTAKEN, I'M AFRAID...
THIS ONE HAS SOME STRANGE IDEAS!
THE MALE EARTHLING HAS NOTHING TO SAY?
NO.
THE CONTENTS OF HIS BOX SEEM TO AGREE, THOUGH ...
THE ARMS DELIVERY THAT BLASTED KATUBIAN PROMISED DID INCLUDE THREE UNEMPLOYED SO-CALLED ARTISTS...
NOT UNEMPLOYED! CERTAINLY NOT! VICTIMS OF A CONSPIRACY, RATHER!!
WHOA THERE...
THREE RENOWNED ARTISTS, THEN... THREE ARTISTS RECRUITED BECAUSE OF THEIR PARTICULAR PHYSICAL ABILITIES – WHICH I'D LIKE TO LEARN MORE ABOUT, EVEN THOUGH I HAD A GLIMPSE YESTERDAY...
DID YOU LIKE IT?
IF YOU MEAN A SHOW...
A SHOW, BUT UNDER CERTAIN CONDITIONS...
AND ALSO A FOURTH, ESPECIALLY EFFECTIVE DELIVERY. I DON'T SEE IT HERE, THOUGH. UNLESS... LET ME GUESS.
CAN I SEE WHAT'S IN THERE?
IF YOU WANT...
29

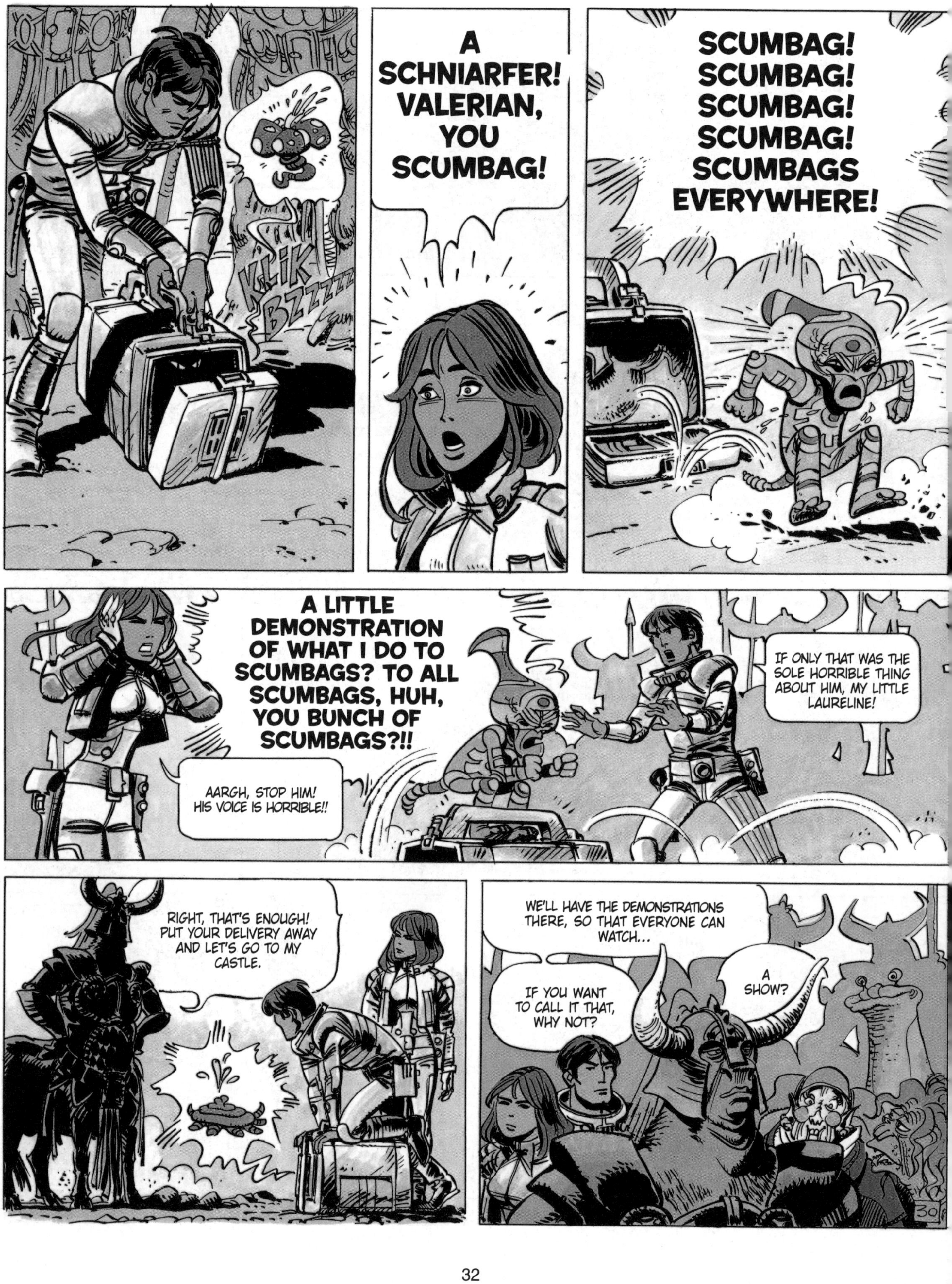
KLIK
BZZZZZ
A SCHNIARFER! VALERIAN, YOU SCUMBAG!
SCUMBAG! SCUMBAG! SCUMBAG! SCUMBAG! SCUMBAGS EVERYWHERE!
A LITTLE DEMONSTRATION OF WHAT I DO TO SCUMBAGS? TO ALL SCUMBAGS, HUH, YOU BUNCH OF SCUMBAGS?!!
AARGH, STOP HIM! HIS VOICE IS HORRIBLE!!
IF ONLY THAT WAS THE SOLE HORRIBLE THING ABOUT HIM, MY LITTLE LAURELINE!
RIGHT, THAT'S ENOUGH! PUT YOUR DELIVERY AWAY AND LET'S GO TO MY CASTLE.
WE'LL HAVE THE DEMONSTRATIONS THERE, SO THAT EVERYONE CAN WATCH...
A SHOW?
IF YOU WANT TO CALL IT THAT, WHY NOT?
30

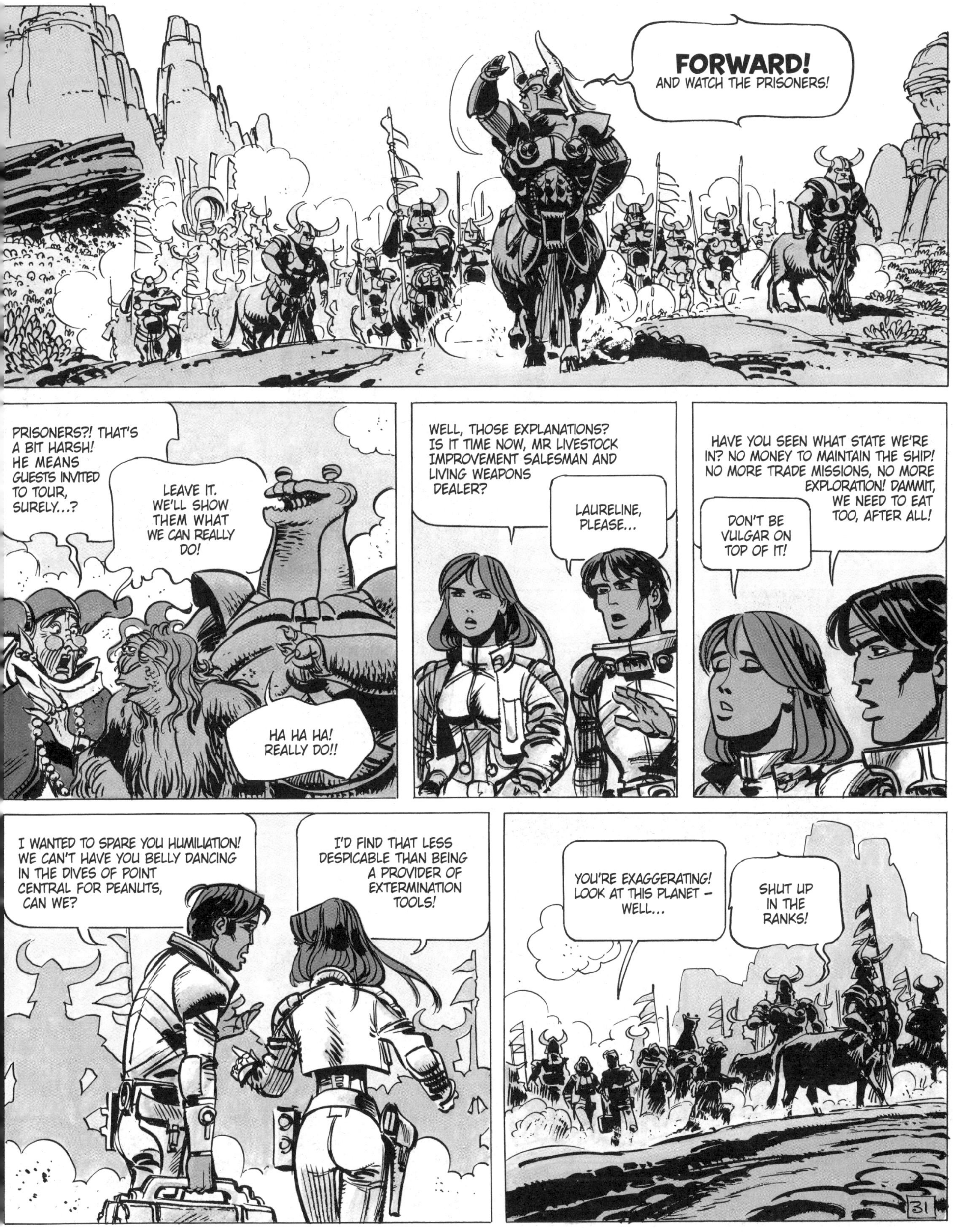
FORWARD!
AND WATCH THE PRISONERS!
PRISONERS?! THAT'S A BIT HARSH! HE MEANS GUESTS INVITED TO TOUR, SURELY...?
LEAVE IT. WE'LL SHOW THEM WHAT WE CAN REALLY DO!
HA HA HA! REALLY DO!!
WELL, THOSE EXPLANATIONS? IS IT TIME NOW, MR LIVESTOCK IMPROVEMENT SALESMAN AND LIVING WEAPONS DEALER?
LAURELINE, PLEASE...
HAVE YOU SEEN WHAT STATE WE'RE IN? NO MONEY TO MAINTAIN THE SHIP! NO MORE TRADE MISSIONS, NO MORE EXPLORATION! DAMMIT, WE NEED TO EAT TOO, AFTER ALL!
DON'T BE VULGAR ON TOP OF IT!
I WANTED TO SPARE YOU HUMILIATION! WE CAN'T HAVE YOU BELLY DANCING IN THE DIVES OF POINT CENTRAL FOR PEANUTS, CAN WE?
I'D FIND THAT LESS DESPICABLE THAN BEING A PROVIDER OF EXTERMINATION TOOLS!
YOU'RE EXAGGERATING! LOOK AT THIS PLANET – WELL...
SHUT UP IN THE RANKS!
31

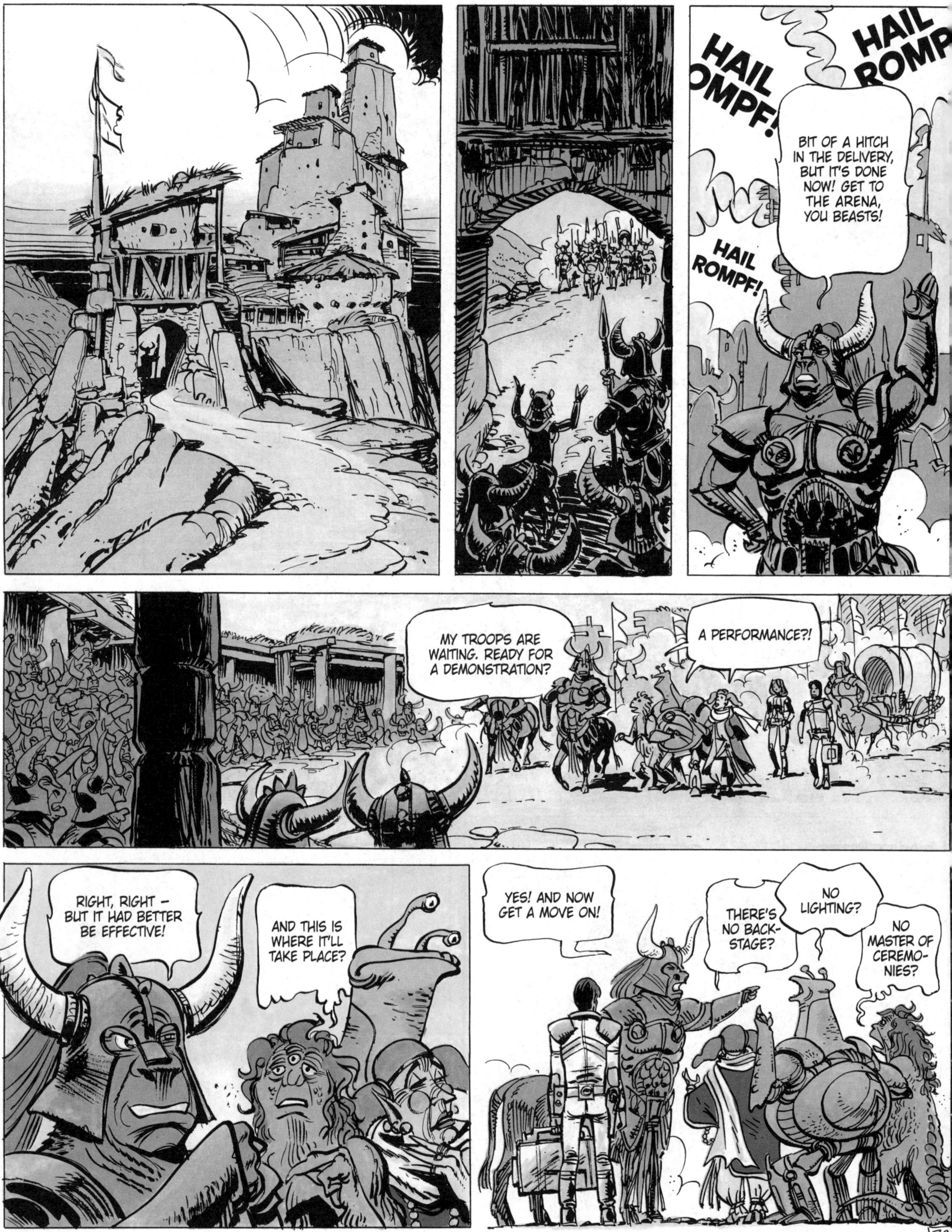
HAIL ROMPF!
HAIL ROMPF!
BIT OF A HITCH IN THE DELIVERY, BUT IT'S DONE NOW! GET TO THE ARENA, YOU BEASTS!
HAIL ROMPF!
MY TROOPS ARE WAITING. READY FOR A DEMONSTRATION?
A PERFORMANCE?!
RIGHT, RIGHT – BUT IT HAD BETTER BE EFFECTIVE!
AND THIS IS WHERE IT'LL TAKE PLACE?
YES! AND NOW GET A MOVE ON!
THERE'S NO BACK-STAGE?
NO LIGHTING?
NO MASTER OF CEREMO-NIES?
32

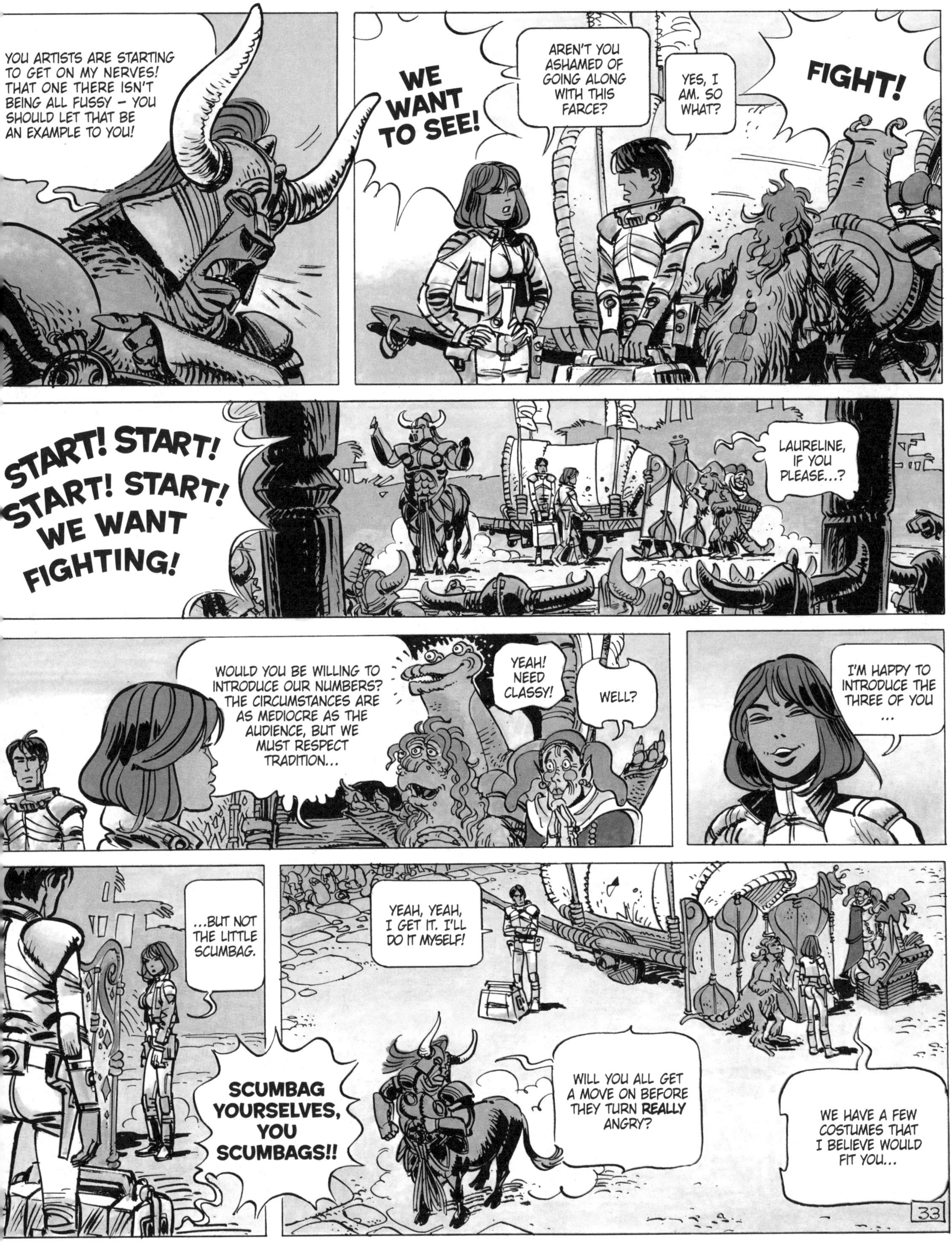

YOU ARTISTS ARE STARTING TO GET ON MY NERVES! THAT ONE THERE ISN'T BEING ALL FUSSY – YOU SHOULD LET THAT BE AN EXAMPLE TO YOU!
WE WANT TO SEE!
AREN'T YOU ASHAMED OF GOING ALONG WITH THIS FARCE?
YES, I AM. SO WHAT?
FIGHT!
START! START! START! START! WE WANT FIGHTING!
LAURELINE, IF YOU PLEASE...?
WOULD YOU BE WILLING TO INTRODUCE OUR NUMBERS? THE CIRCUMSTANCES ARE AS MEDIOCRE AS THE AUDIENCE, BUT WE MUST RESPECT TRADITION...
YEAH! NEED CLASSY!
WELL?
I'M HAPPY TO INTRODUCE THE THREE OF YOU ...
...BUT NOT THE LITTLE SCUMBAG.
SCUMBAG YOURSELVES, YOU SCUMBAGS!!
YEAH, YEAH, I GET IT. I'LL DO IT MYSELF!
WILL YOU ALL GET A MOVE ON BEFORE THEY TURN REALLY ANGRY?
WE HAVE A FEW COSTUMES THAT I BELIEVE WOULD FIT YOU...
33

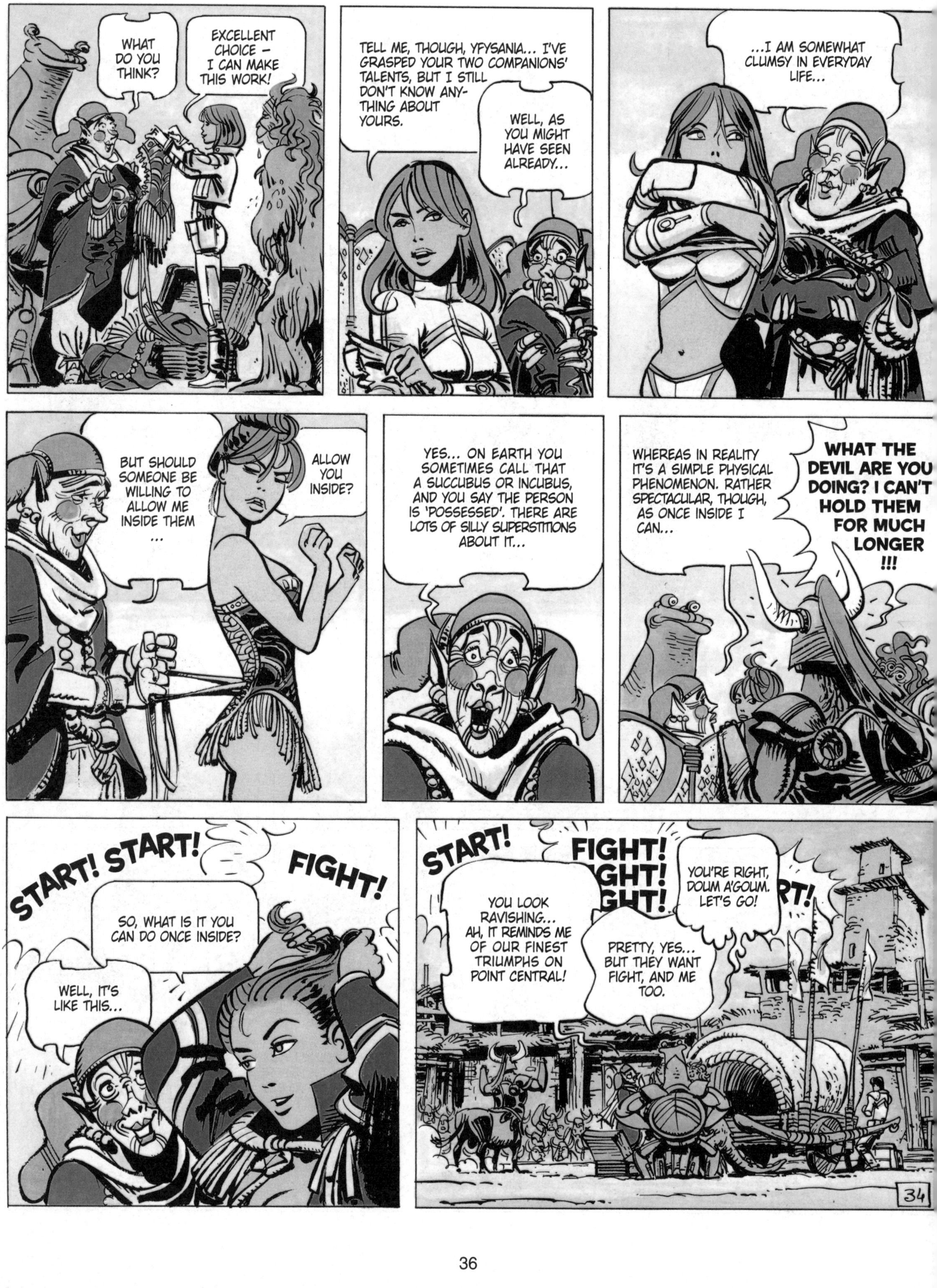
WHAT DO YOU THINK?
EXCELLENT CHOICE – I CAN MAKE THIS WORK!
TELL ME, THOUGH, YFYSANIA... I'VE GRASPED YOUR TWO COMPANIONS' TALENTS, BUT I STILL DON'T KNOW ANYTHING ABOUT YOURS.
WELL, AS YOU MIGHT HAVE SEEN ALREADY...
...I AM SOMEWHAT CLUMSY IN EVERYDAY LIFE...
BUT SHOULD SOMEONE BE WILLING TO ALLOW ME INSIDE THEM ...
ALLOW YOU INSIDE?
YES... ON EARTH YOU SOMETIMES CALL THAT A SUCCUBUS OR INCUBUS, AND YOU SAY THE PERSON IS 'POSSESSED'. THERE ARE LOTS OF SILLY SUPERSTITIONS ABOUT IT...
WHEREAS IN REALITY IT'S A SIMPLE PHYSICAL PHENOMENON. RATHER SPECTACULAR, THOUGH, AS ONCE INSIDE I CAN...
WHAT THE DEVIL ARE YOU DOING? I CAN'T HOLD THEM FOR MUCH LONGER !!!
START! START!
FIGHT!
SO, WHAT IS IT YOU CAN DO ONCE INSIDE?
WELL, IT'S LIKE THIS...
START!
FIGHT!
YOU LOOK RAVISHING... AH, IT REMINDS ME OF OUR FINEST TRIUMPHS ON POINT CENTRAL!
YOU'RE RIGHT, DOUM A'GOUM. LET'S GO!
PRETTY, YES... BUT THEY WANT FIGHT, AND ME TOO.
34

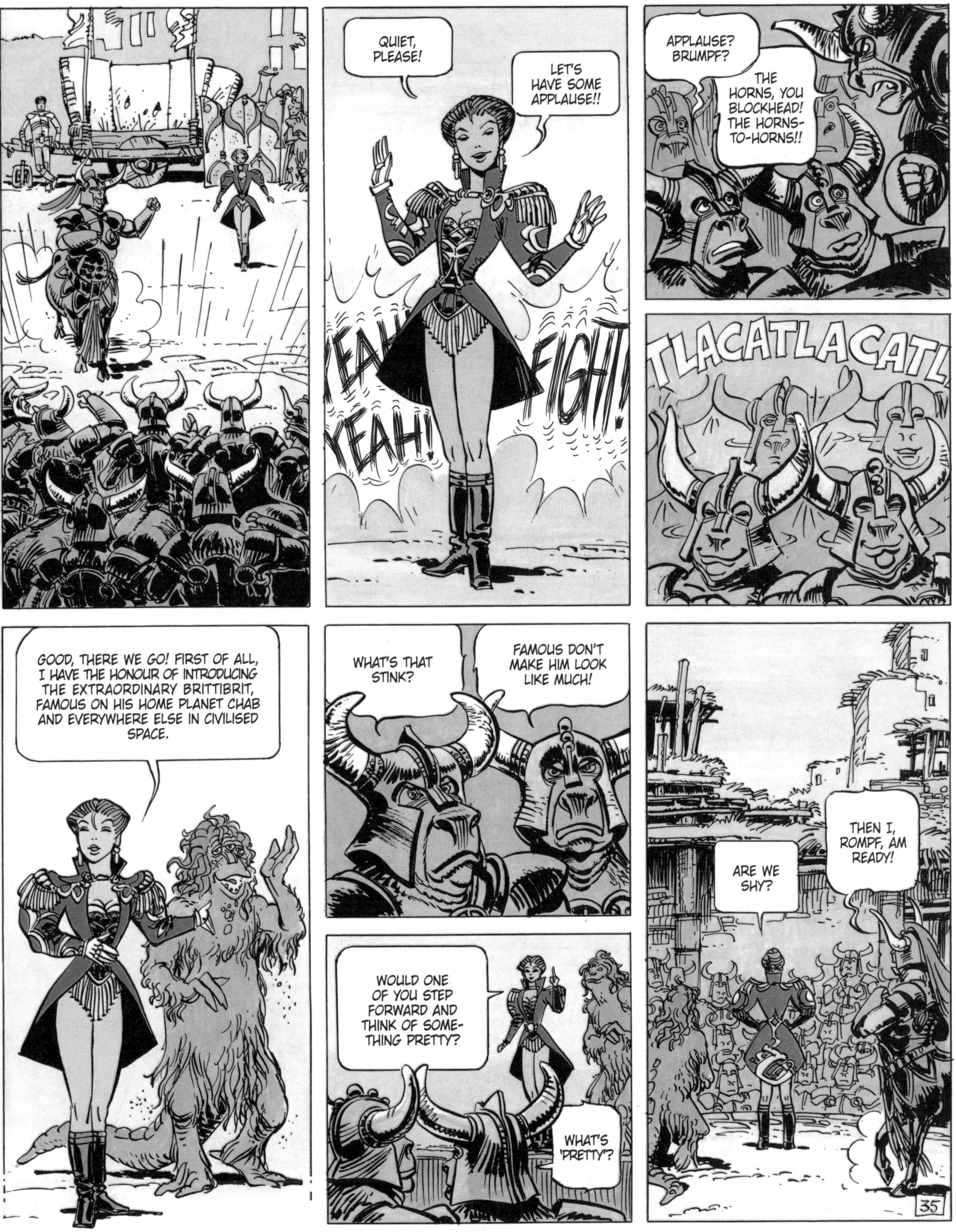
QUIET, PLEASE!
LET'S HAVE SOME APPLAUSE!!
YEAH! YEAH! FIGHT!
APPLAUSE? BRUMPF?
THE HORNS, YOU BLOCKHEAD! THE HORNS-TO-HORNS!!
TLACATLACATL
GOOD, THERE WE GO! FIRST OF ALL, I HAVE THE HONOUR OF INTRODUCING THE EXTRAORDINARY BRITTIBRIT, FAMOUS ON HIS HOME PLANET CHAB AND EVERYWHERE ELSE IN CIVILISED SPACE.
WHAT'S THAT STINK?
FAMOUS DON'T MAKE HIM LOOK LIKE MUCH!
WOULD ONE OF YOU STEP FORWARD AND THINK OF SOMETHING PRETTY?
WHAT'S 'PRETTY'?
ARE WE SHY?
THEN I, ROMPF, AM READY!
35

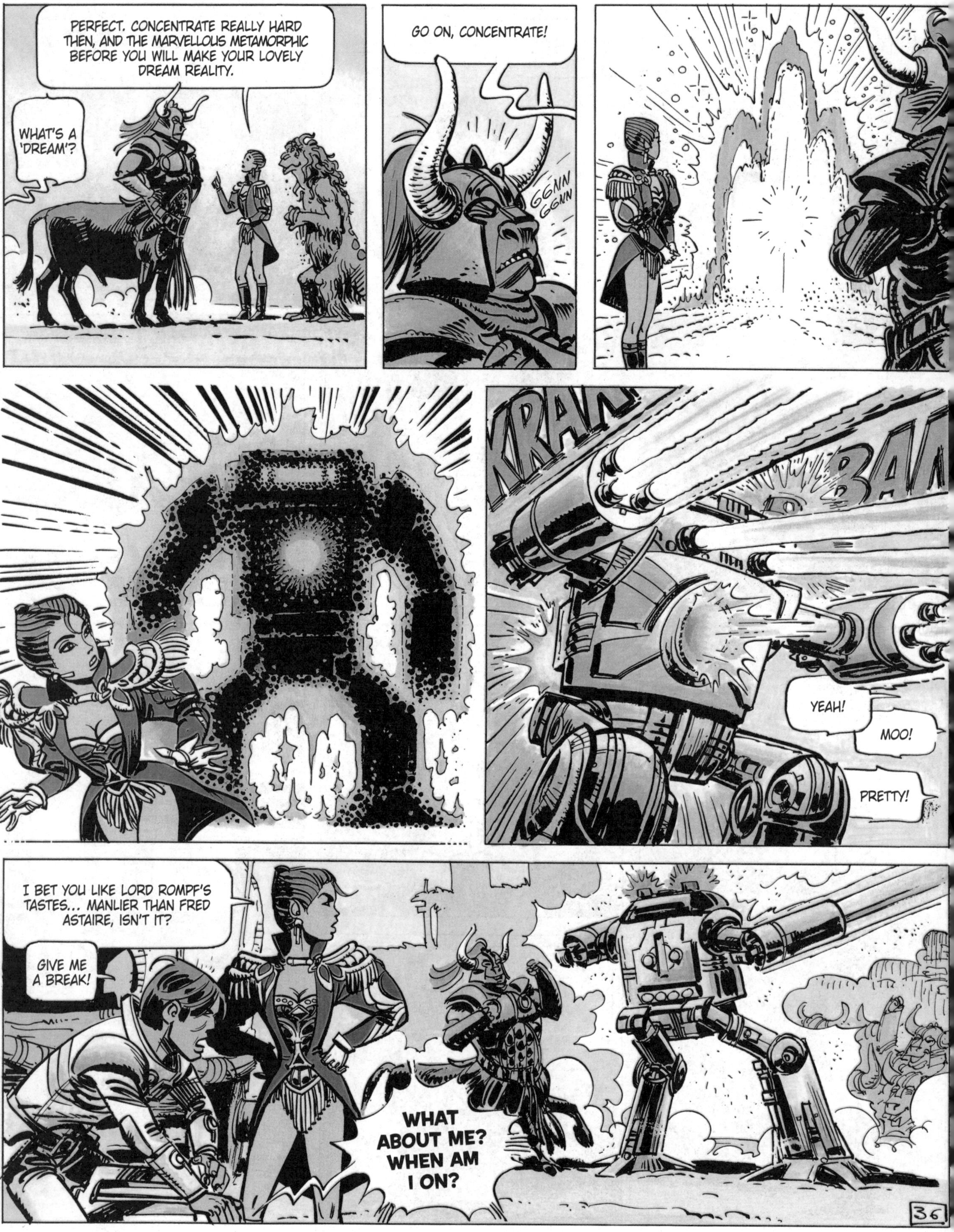
PERFECT. CONCENTRATE REALLY HARD THEN, AND THE MARVELLOUS METAMORPHIC BEFORE YOU WILL MAKE YOUR LOVELY DREAM REALITY.
WHAT'S A 'DREAM'?
GO ON, CONCENTRATE!
GGNN GGNN
KRAK
BAM
YEAH!
MOO!
PRETTY!
I BET YOU LIKE LORD ROMPF'S TASTES... MANLIER THAN FRED ASTAIRE, ISN'T IT?
GIVE ME A BREAK!
WHAT ABOUT ME? WHEN AM I ON?
36.

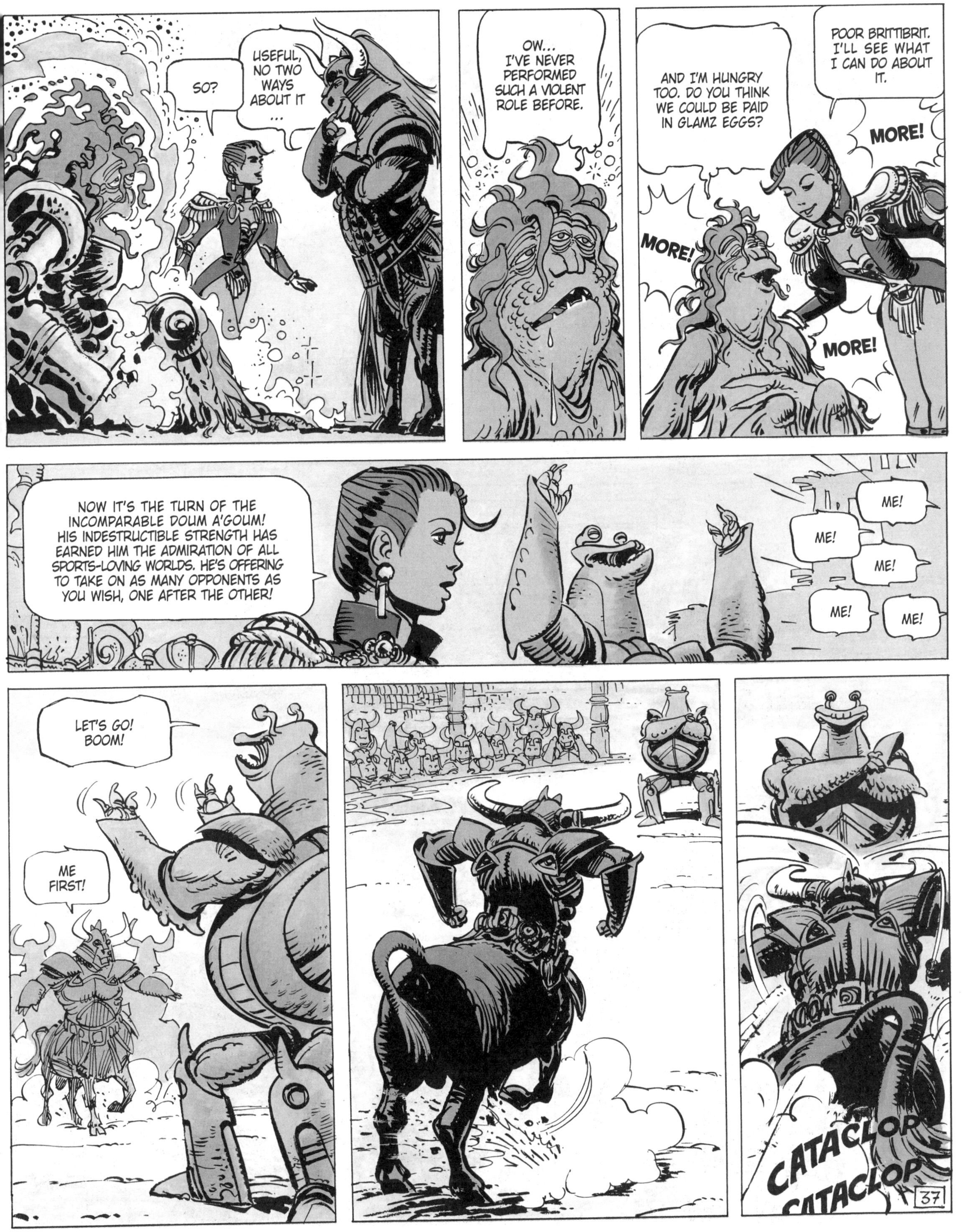
SO?
USEFUL, NO TWO WAYS ABOUT IT ...
OW... I'VE NEVER PERFORMED SUCH A VIOLENT ROLE BEFORE.
AND I'M HUNGRY TOO. DO YOU THINK WE COULD BE PAID IN GLAMZ EGGS?
POOR BRITTIBRIT. I'LL SEE WHAT I CAN DO ABOUT IT.
MORE!
MORE!
MORE!
NOW IT'S THE TURN OF THE INCOMPARABLE DOUM A'GOUM! HIS INDESTRUCTIBLE STRENGTH HAS EARNED HIM THE ADMIRATION OF ALL SPORTS-LOVING WORLDS. HE'S OFFERING TO TAKE ON AS MANY OPPONENTS AS YOU WISH, ONE AFTER THE OTHER!
ME!
ME!
ME!
ME!
ME!
LET'S GO! BOOM!
ME FIRST!
CATACLOP
CATACLOP
37

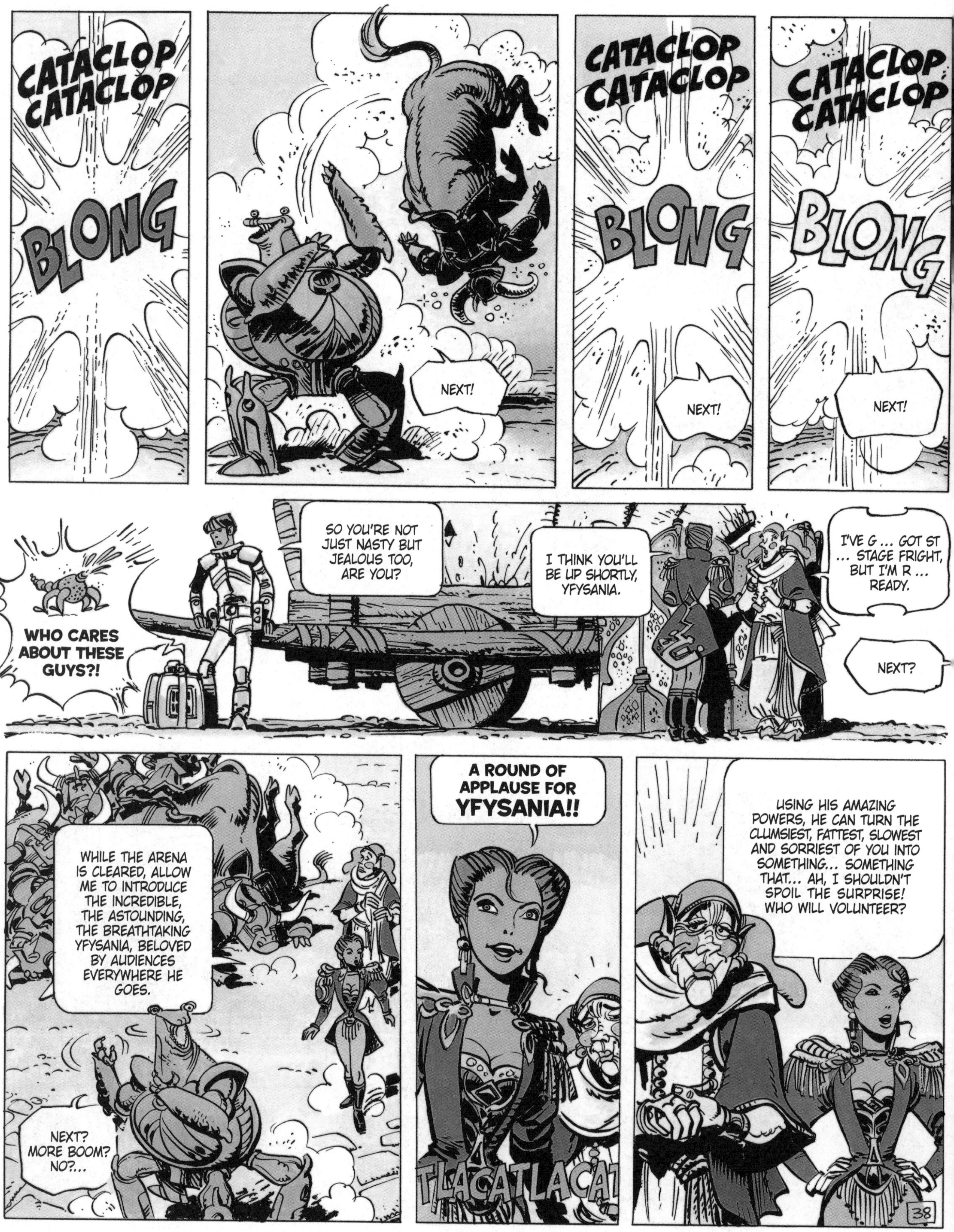
CATACLOP CATACLOP
BLONG
NEXT!
CATACLOP CATACLOP
BLONG
NEXT!
CATACLOP CATACLOP
BLONG
NEXT!
WHO CARES ABOUT THESE GUYS?!
SO YOU'RE NOT JUST NASTY BUT JEALOUS TOO, ARE YOU?
I THINK YOU'LL BE UP SHORTLY, YFYSANIA.
I'VE G ... GOT ST ... STAGE FRIGHT, BUT I'M R ... READY.
NEXT?
WHILE THE ARENA IS CLEARED, ALLOW ME TO INTRODUCE THE INCREDIBLE, THE ASTOUNDING, THE BREATHTAKING YFYSANIA, BELOVED BY AUDIENCES EVERYWHERE HE GOES.
NEXT? MORE BOOM? NO?...
A ROUND OF APPLAUSE FOR YFYSANIA!!
TLACATLACAT
USING HIS AMAZING POWERS, HE CAN TURN THE CLUMSIEST, FATTEST, SLOWEST AND SORRIEST OF YOU INTO SOMETHING... SOMETHING THAT... AH, I SHOULDN'T SPOIL THE SURPRISE! WHO WILL VOLUNTEER?
38

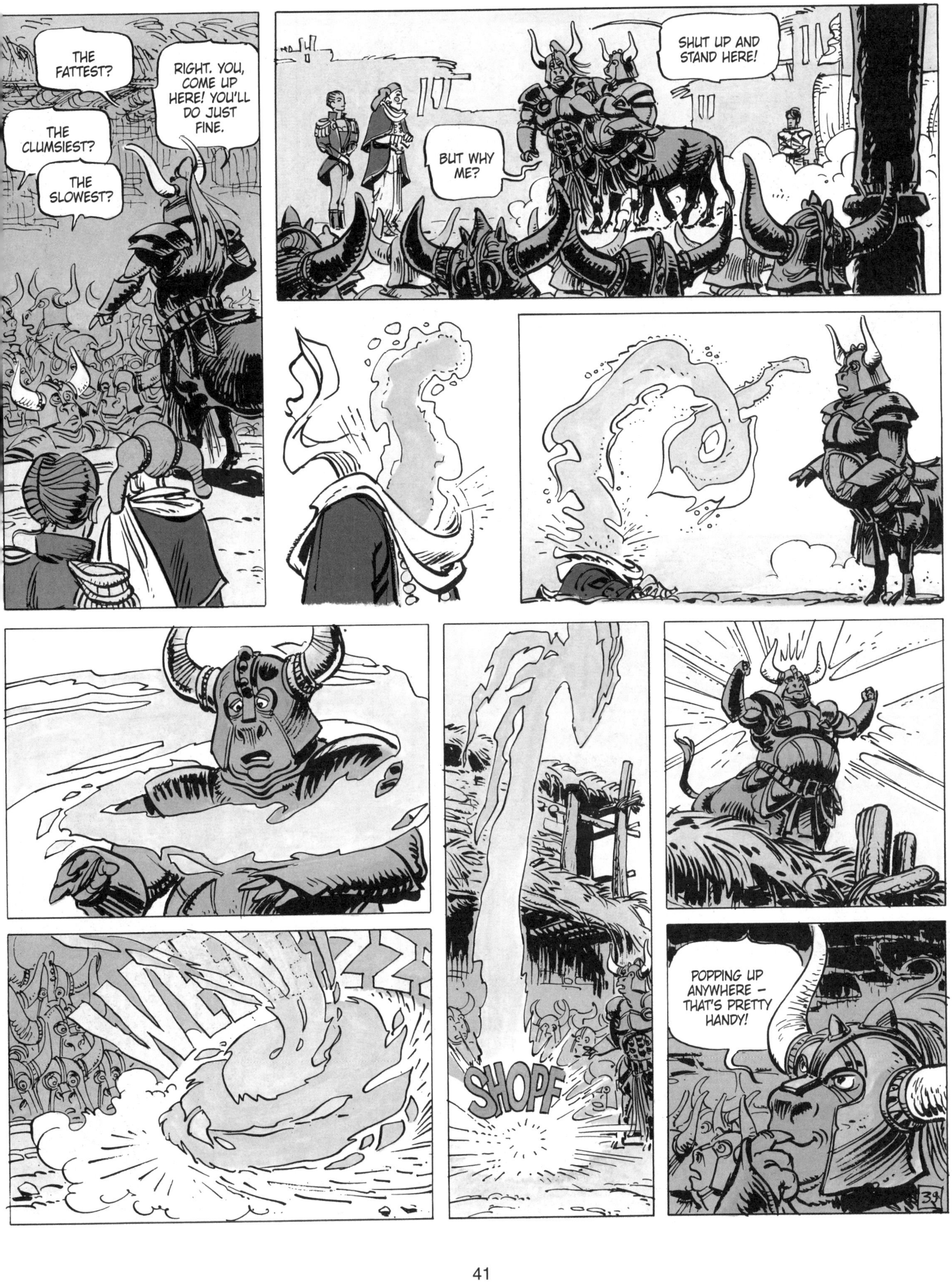

THE FATTEST?
THE CLUMSIEST?
THE SLOWEST?
RIGHT. YOU, COME UP HERE! YOU'LL DO JUST FINE.
SHUT UP AND STAND HERE!
BUT WHY ME?
SHOPF
POPPING UP ANYWHERE – THAT'S PRETTY HANDY!
39

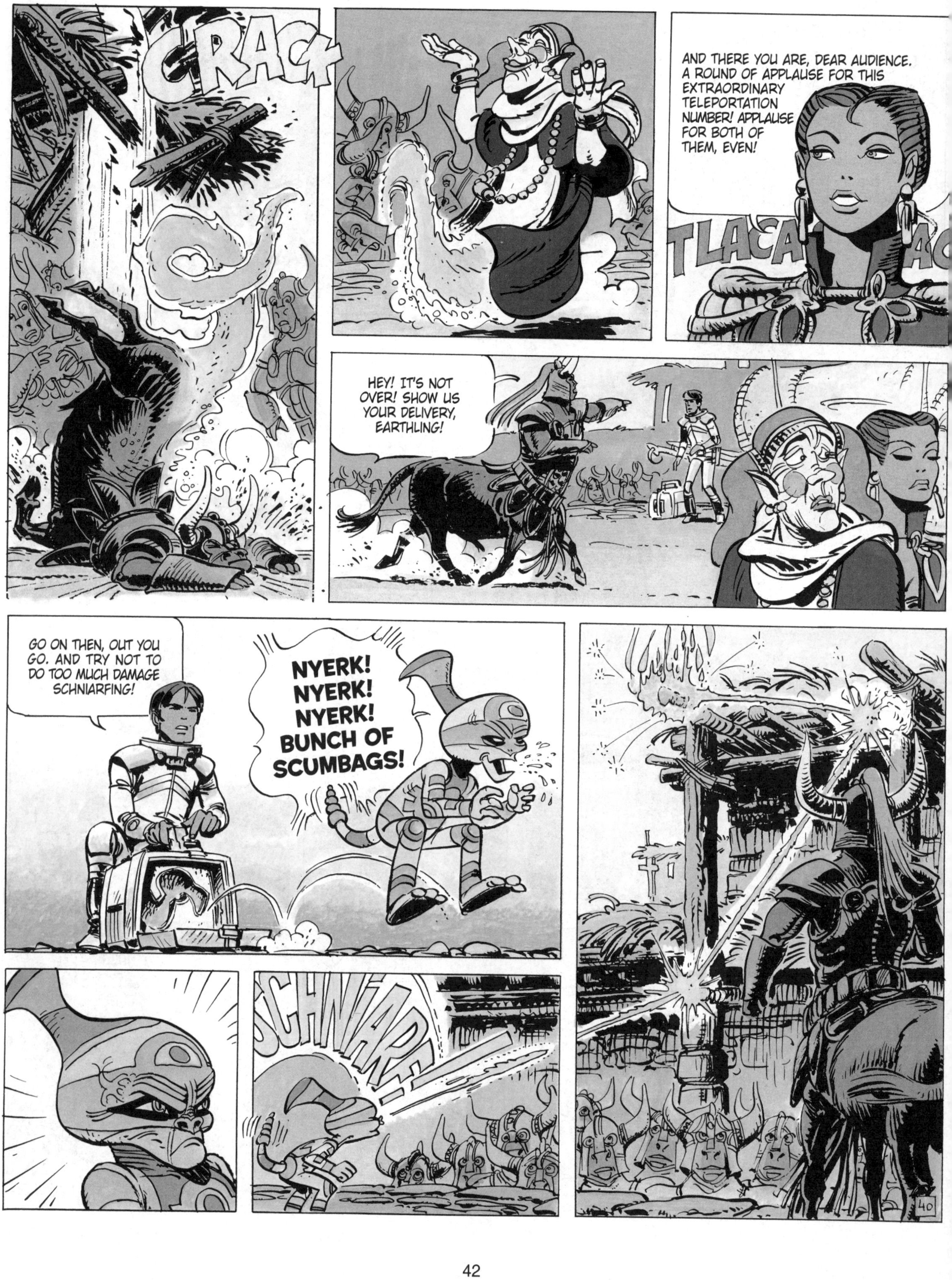
CRACK
AND THERE YOU ARE, DEAR AUDIENCE. A ROUND OF APPLAUSE FOR THIS EXTRAORDINARY TELEPORTATION NUMBER! APPLAUSE FOR BOTH OF THEM, EVEN!
TLACA
HEY! IT'S NOT OVER! SHOW US YOUR DELIVERY, EARTHLING!
GO ON THEN, OUT YOU GO. AND TRY NOT TO DO TOO MUCH DAMAGE SCHNIARFING!
NYERK! NYERK! NYERK! BUNCH OF SCUMBAGS!
SCHNIARF!
40

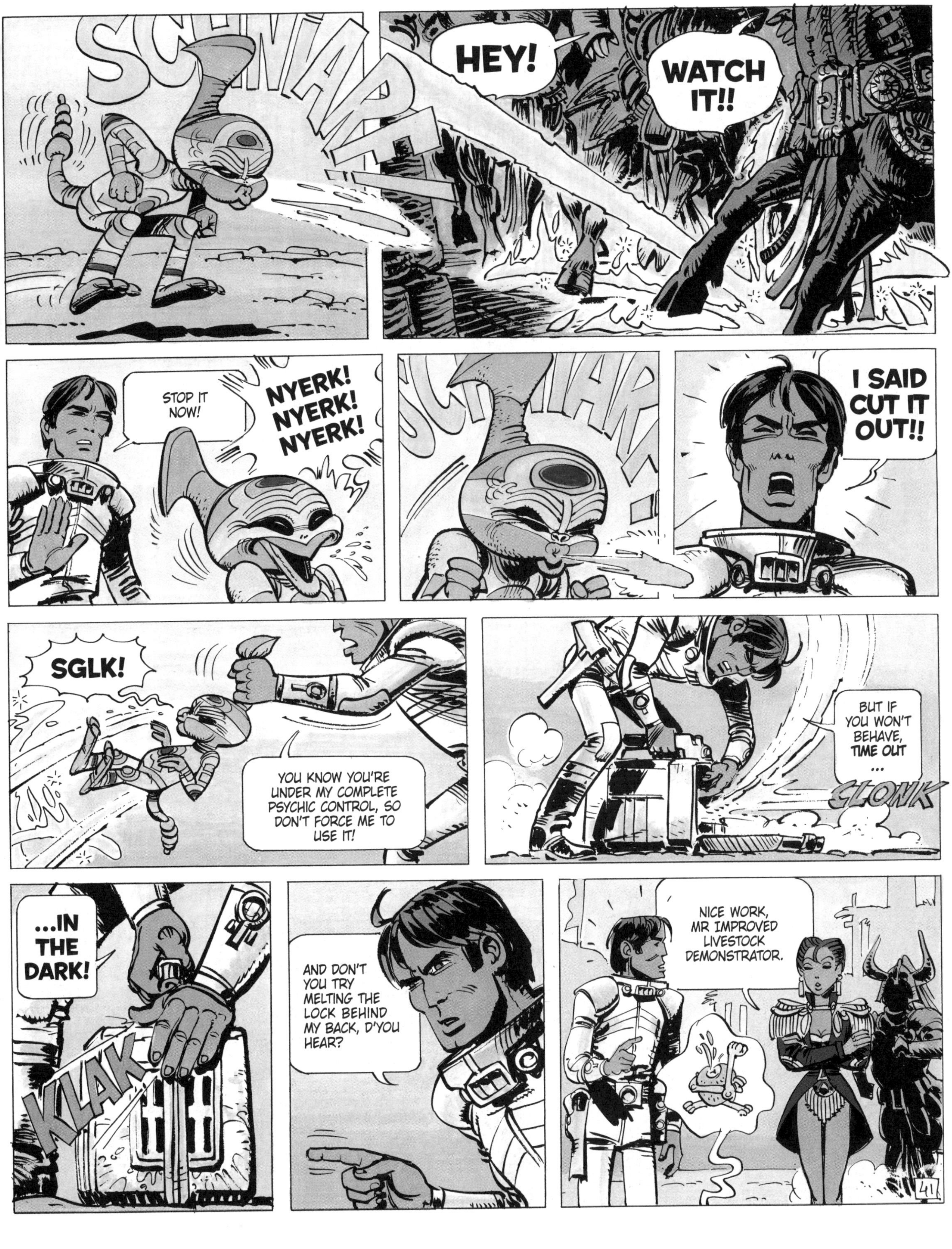
SCHNIARF
HEY!
WATCH IT!!
STOP IT NOW!
NYERK! NYERK! NYERK!
I SAID CUT IT OUT!!
SGLK!
YOU KNOW YOU'RE UNDER MY COMPLETE PSYCHIC CONTROL, SO DON'T FORCE ME TO USE IT!
BUT IF YOU WON'T BEHAVE, TIME OUT ...
CLONK
...IN THE DARK!
KLAK
AND DON'T YOU TRY MELTING THE LOCK BEHIND MY BACK, D'YOU HEAR?
NICE WORK, MR IMPROVED LIVESTOCK DEMONSTRATOR.
41

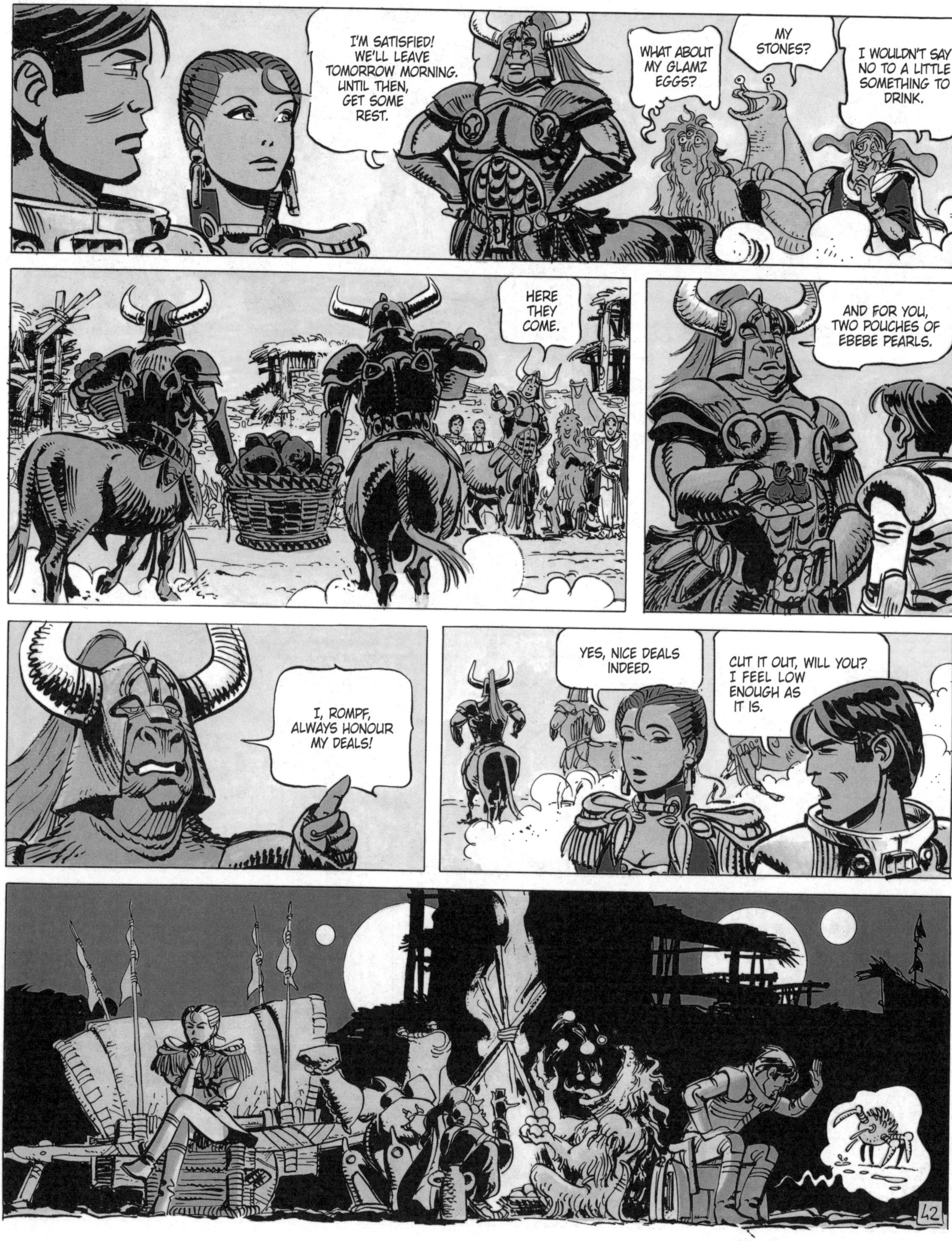
I'M SATISFIED! WE'LL LEAVE TOMORROW MORNING. UNTIL THEN, GET SOME REST.
WHAT ABOUT MY GLAMZ EGGS?
MY STONES?
I WOULDN'T SAY NO TO A LITTLE SOMETHING TO DRINK.
HERE THEY COME.
AND FOR YOU, TWO POUCHES OF EBEBE PEARLS.
I, ROMPF, ALWAYS HONOUR MY DEALS!
YES, NICE DEALS INDEED.
CUT IT OUT, WILL YOU? I FEEL LOW ENOUGH AS IT IS.
42

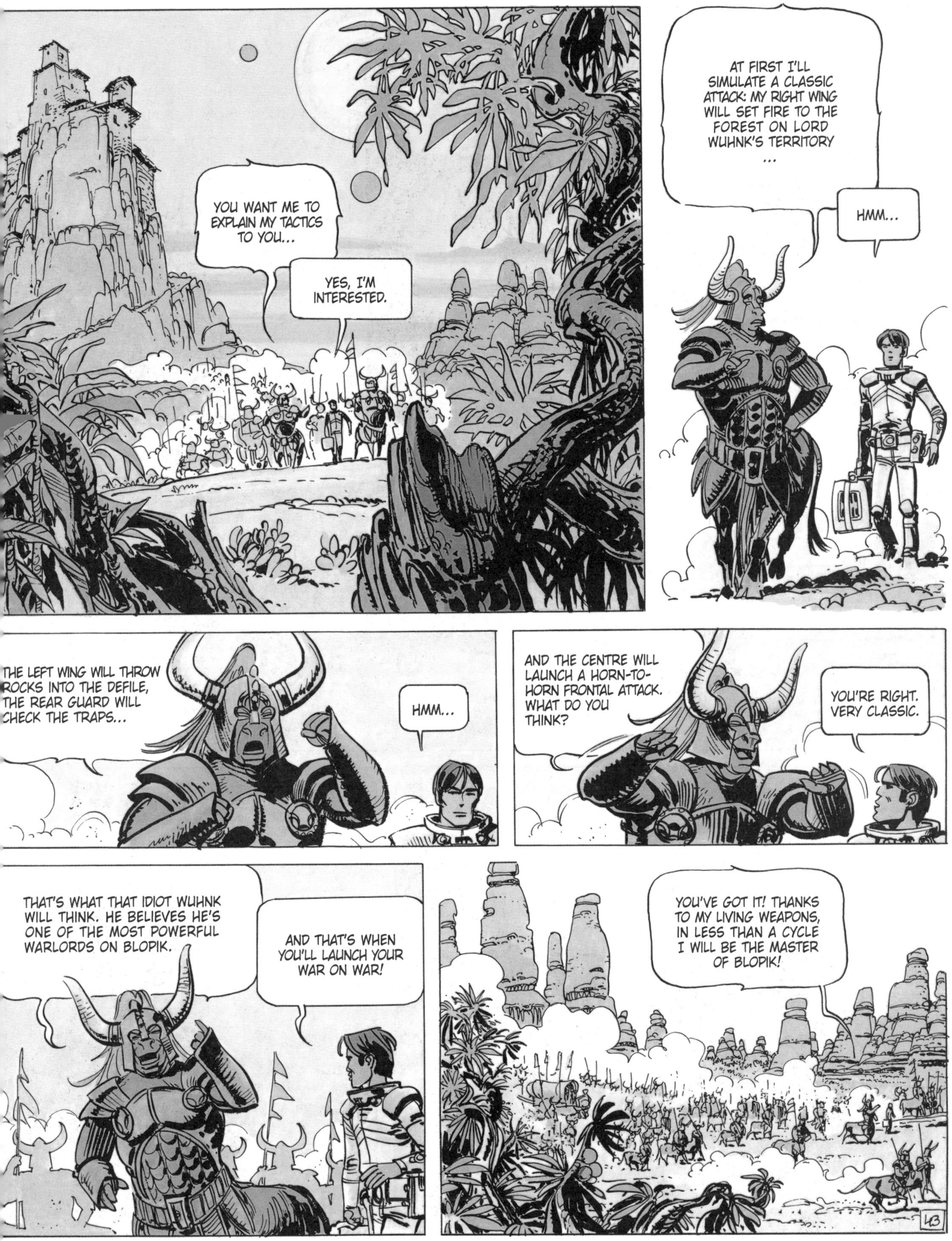
YOU WANT ME TO EXPLAIN MY TACTICS TO YOU...
YES, I'M INTERESTED.
AT FIRST I'LL SIMULATE A CLASSIC ATTACK: MY RIGHT WING WILL SET FIRE TO THE FOREST ON LORD WUHNK'S TERRITORY ...
HMM...
THE LEFT WING WILL THROW ROCKS INTO THE DEFILE, THE REAR GUARD WILL CHECK THE TRAPS...
HMM...
AND THE CENTRE WILL LAUNCH A HORN-TO-HORN FRONTAL ATTACK. WHAT DO YOU THINK?
YOU'RE RIGHT. VERY CLASSIC.
THAT'S WHAT THAT IDIOT WUHNK WILL THINK. HE BELIEVES HE'S ONE OF THE MOST POWERFUL WARLORDS ON BLOPIK.
AND THAT'S WHEN YOU'LL LAUNCH YOUR WAR ON WAR!
YOU'VE GOT IT! THANKS TO MY LIVING WEAPONS, IN LESS THAN A CYCLE I WILL BE THE MASTER OF BLOPIK!

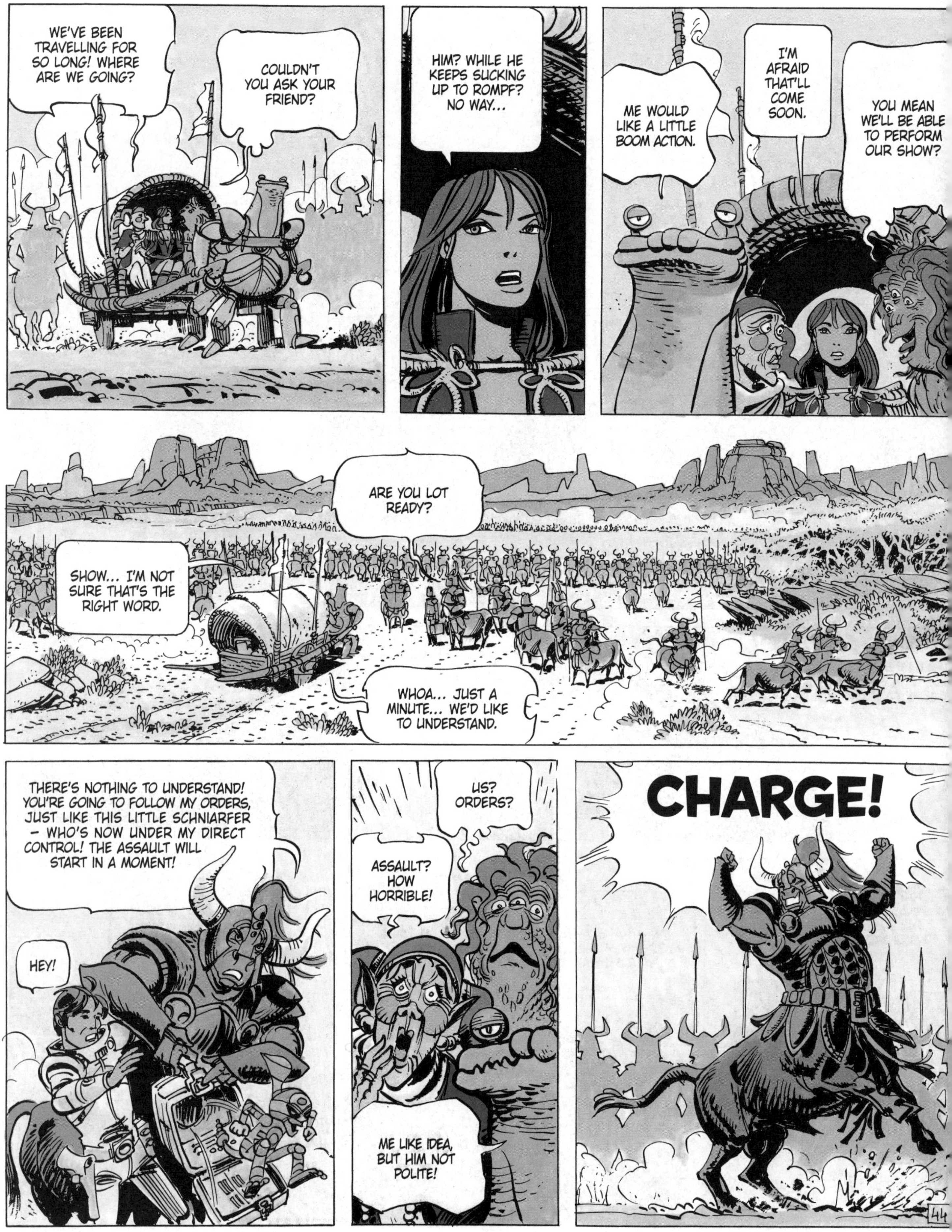
WE'VE BEEN TRAVELLING FOR SO LONG! WHERE ARE WE GOING?
COULDN'T YOU ASK YOUR FRIEND?
HIM? WHILE HE KEEPS SUCKING UP TO ROMPF? NO WAY...
ME WOULD LIKE A LITTLE BOOM ACTION.
I'M AFRAID THAT'LL COME SOON.
YOU MEAN WE'LL BE ABLE TO PERFORM OUR SHOW?
ARE YOU LOT READY?
SHOW... I'M NOT SURE THAT'S THE RIGHT WORD.
WHOA... JUST A MINUTE... WE'D LIKE TO UNDERSTAND.
THERE'S NOTHING TO UNDERSTAND! YOU'RE GOING TO FOLLOW MY ORDERS, JUST LIKE THIS LITTLE SCHNIARFER – WHO'S NOW UNDER MY DIRECT CONTROL! THE ASSAULT WILL START IN A MOMENT!
HEY!
US? ORDERS?
ASSAULT? HOW HORRIBLE!
ME LIKE IDEA, BUT HIM NOT POLITE!
CHARGE!
44

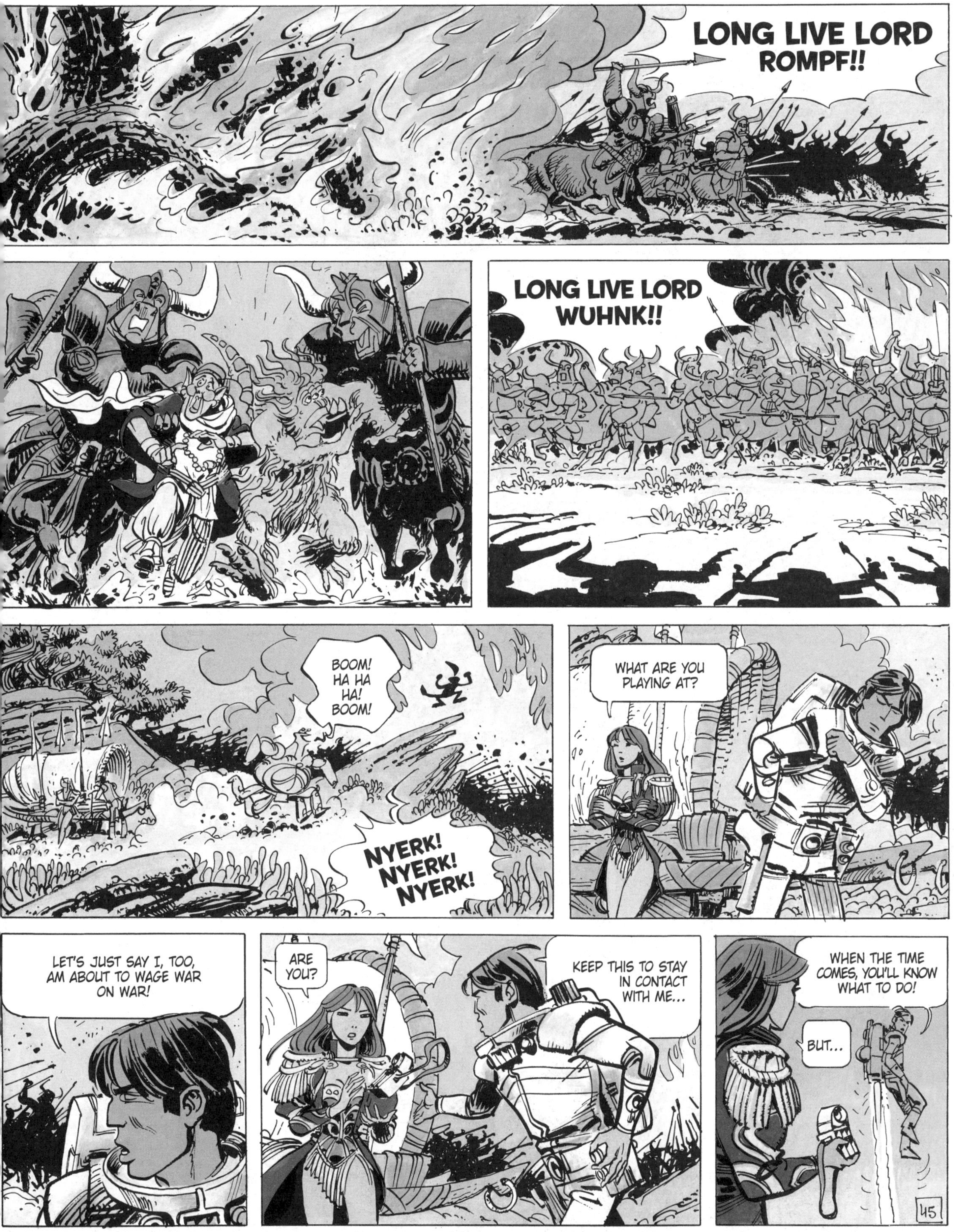
LONG LIVE LORD ROMPF!!
LONG LIVE LORD WUHNK!!
BOOM! HA HA HA! BOOM!
NYERK! NYERK! NYERK!
WHAT ARE YOU PLAYING AT?
LET'S JUST SAY I, TOO, AM ABOUT TO WAGE WAR ON WAR!
ARE YOU?
KEEP THIS TO STAY IN CONTACT WITH ME...
WHEN THE TIME COMES, YOU'LL KNOW WHAT TO DO!
BUT...
45

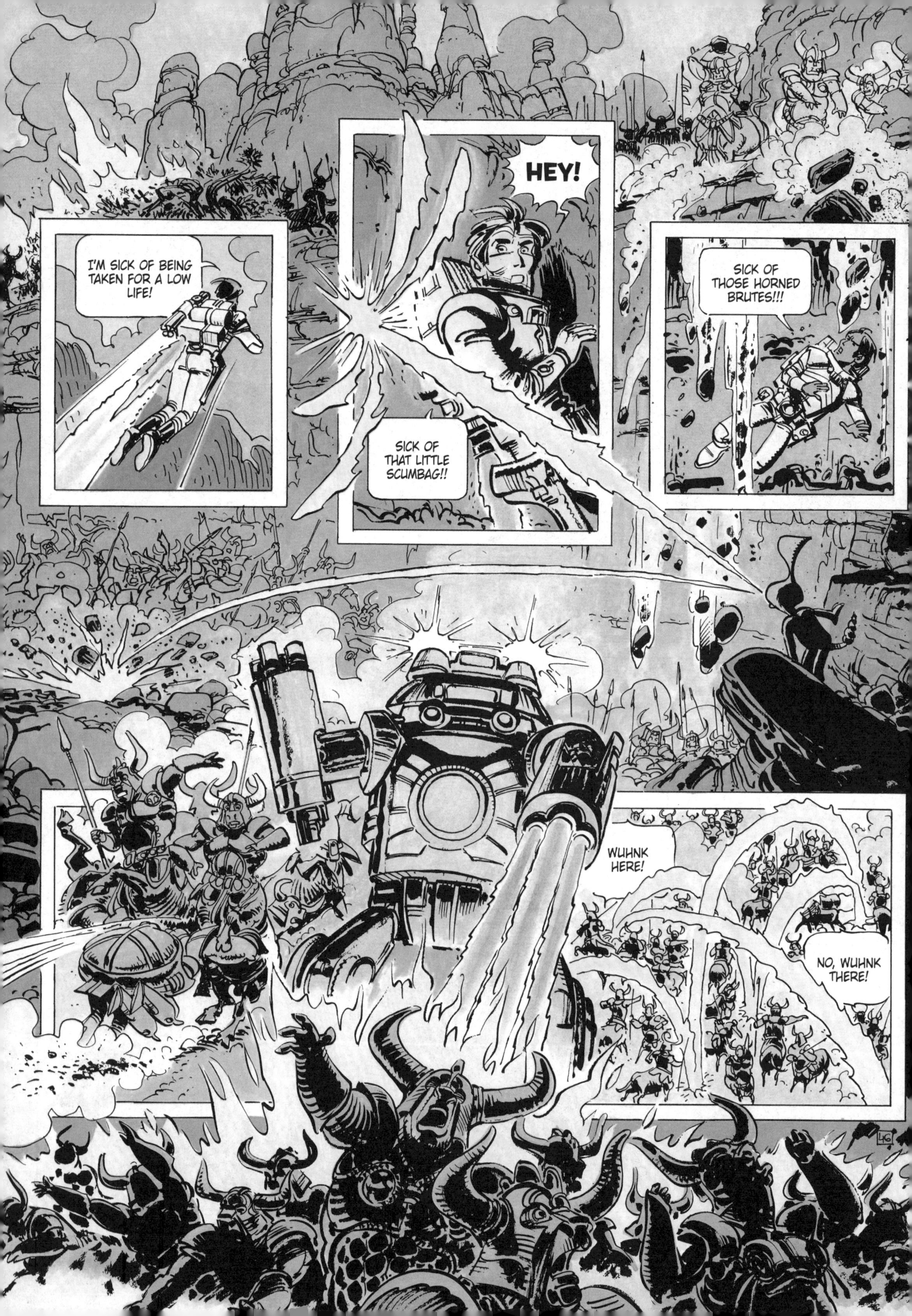
I'M SICK OF BEING TAKEN FOR A LOW LIFE!
HEY!
SICK OF THAT LITTLE SCUMBAG!!
SICK OF THOSE HORNED BRUTES!!!
WUHNK HERE!
NO, WUHNK THERE!
46

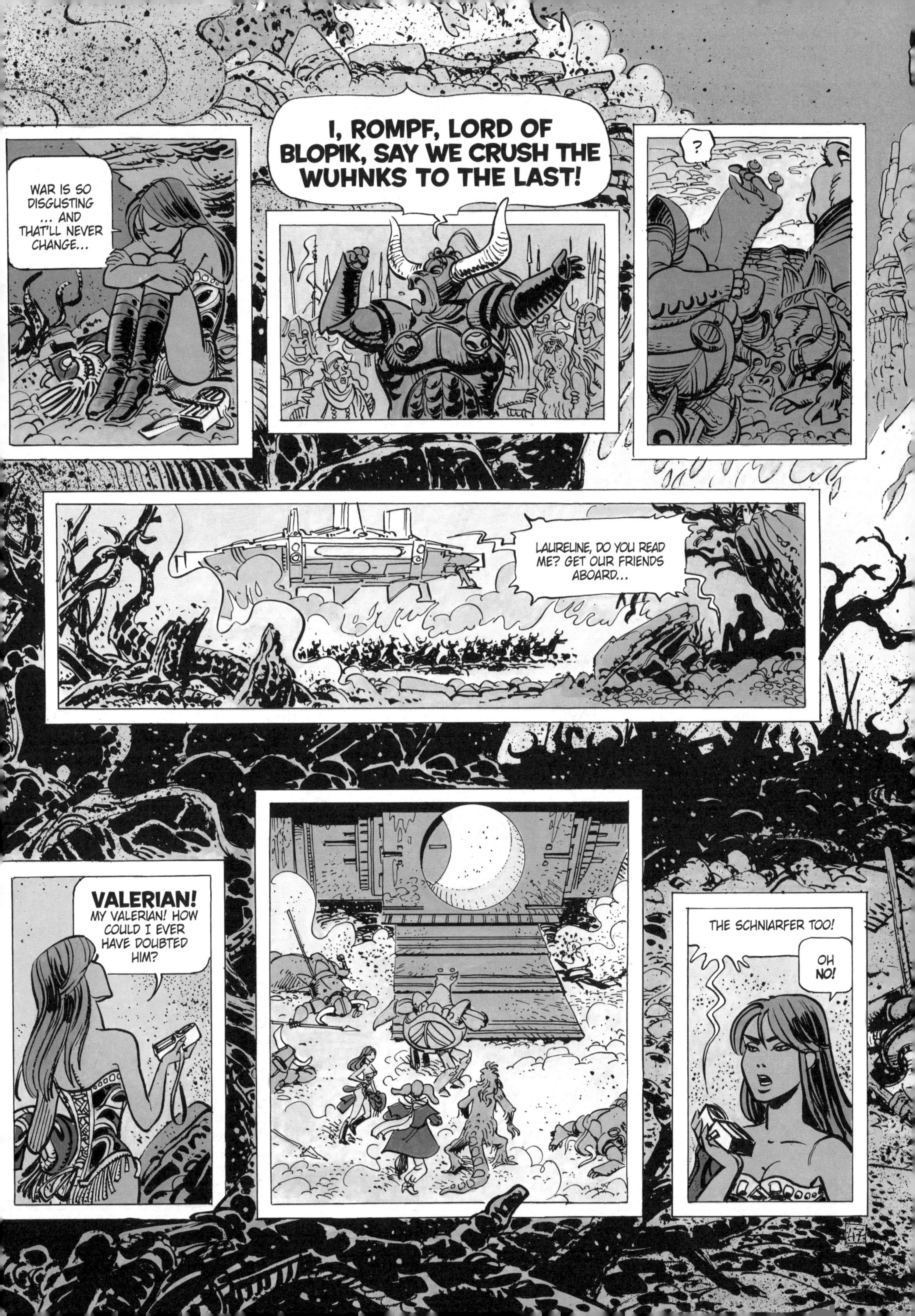

WAR IS SO DISGUSTING ... AND THAT'LL NEVER CHANGE...
I, ROMPF, LORD OF BLOPIK, SAY WE CRUSH THE WUHNKS TO THE LAST!
?
LAURELINE, DO YOU READ ME? GET OUR FRIENDS ABOARD...
VALERIAN! MY VALERIAN! HOW COULD I EVER HAVE DOUBTED HIM?
THE SCHNIARFER TOO!
OH NO!

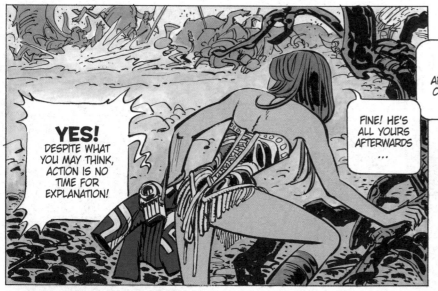

YES! DESPITE WHAT YOU MAY THINK, ACTION IS NO TIME FOR EXPLANATION!

FINE! HE'S ALL YOURS AFTERWARDS...

I KNOW ABOUT PSYCHIC CONTROL TOO!

EVERYONE! THE SHIP IS ON THE BLINK, SO HOLD ON TO SOMETHING!!

YOU SCUMBAGS! IT'S BECAUSE OF YOU THAT BLOPIK WILL NEVER BE AT PEACE...

THAT'S ENOUGH TO PUT A WARLORD OFF WAGING WAR ON WAR!

SCUMB... OUCH!

AAAAA

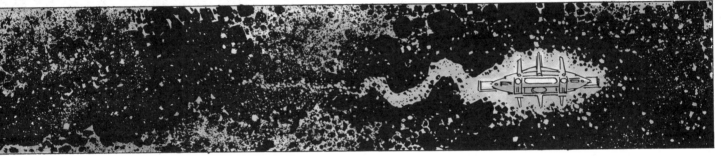

I THINK THE PROCEDURE WAS A SUCCESS!

I'M NOT TOO KEEN ON YOU MEDDLING IN GENETIC MANIPULATIONS.

BE FAIR, WILL YOU! WHAT I'M DOING IS REVERSIBLE. IF HE DOESN'T LIKE IT, OR YOU, WE CAN UNBIND HIS SHABLINAL GLAND.

LOOK! HE'S COMING TO.

HEYO!

HELLO! HOW ARE YOU DOING, MY FRIENDS?

ER... WELL, YOU'RE THE ONE WHO...

I'M PERFECTLY ALL RIGHT, MY DEAR LAURELINE... TO TELL YOU THE TRUTH, I'VE NEVER TAKEN ANY PARTICULAR PLEASURE IN BEING NASTY. BUT WE SCHNIARFERS COME FROM BROMN, A HORRIBLY DANGEROUS PLANET, YOU SEE. MATTER-EATING BEASTS, VOID HOUNDS, SPLITTING SHALAFUTS... WE ARE SPARED VERY LITTLE, I'M AFRAID...

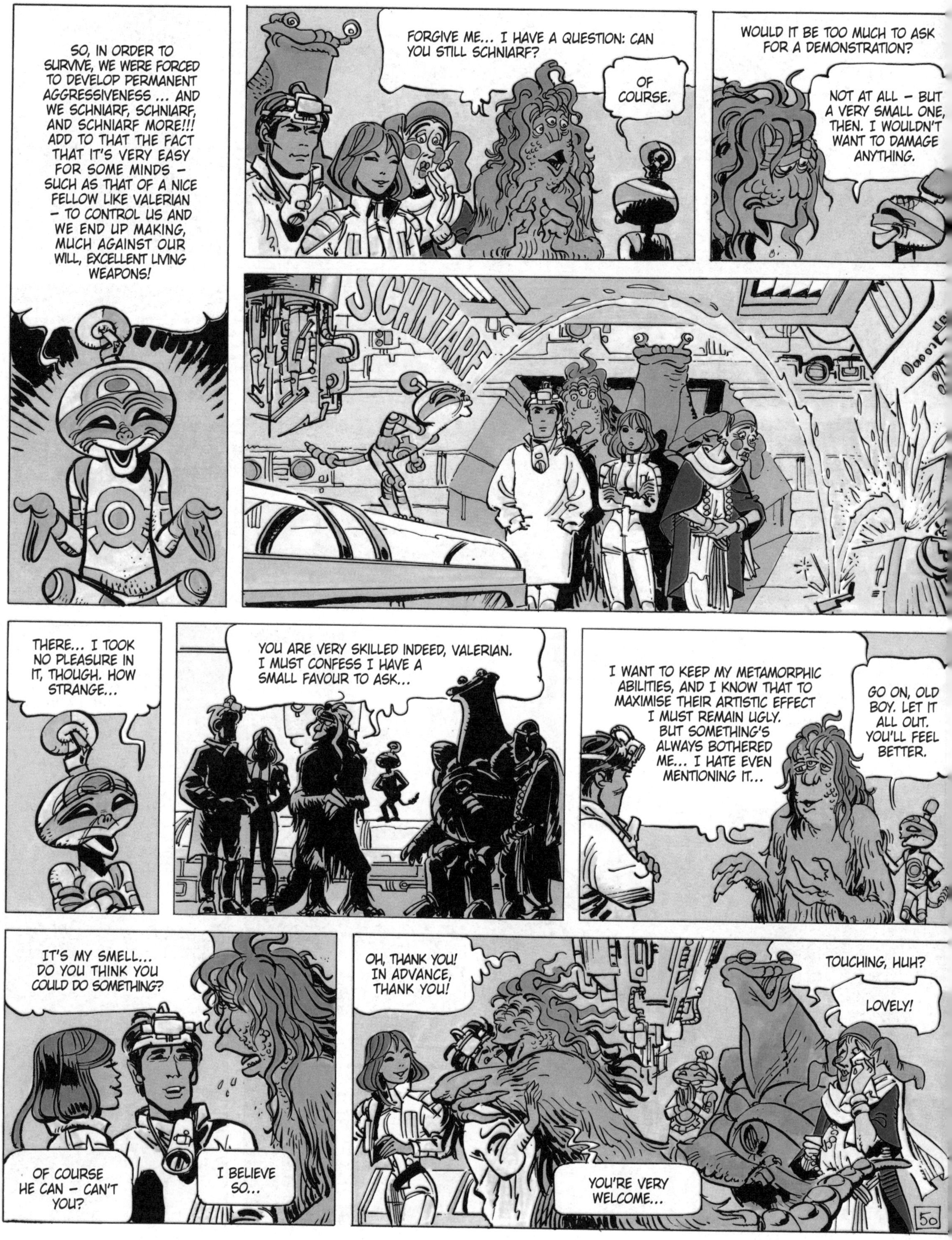
SO, IN ORDER TO SURVIVE, WE WERE FORCED TO DEVELOP PERMANENT AGGRESSIVENESS ... AND WE SCHNIARF, SCHNIARF, AND SCHNIARF MORE!!! ADD TO THAT THE FACT THAT IT'S VERY EASY FOR SOME MINDS – SUCH AS THAT OF A NICE FELLOW LIKE VALERIAN – TO CONTROL US AND WE END UP MAKING, MUCH AGAINST OUR WILL, EXCELLENT LIVING WEAPONS!
FORGIVE ME... I HAVE A QUESTION: CAN YOU STILL SCHNIARF?
OF COURSE.
WOULD IT BE TOO MUCH TO ASK FOR A DEMONSTRATION?
NOT AT ALL – BUT A VERY SMALL ONE, THEN. I WOULDN'T WANT TO DAMAGE ANYTHING.
SCHNIARF
THERE... I TOOK NO PLEASURE IN IT, THOUGH. HOW STRANGE...
YOU ARE VERY SKILLED INDEED, VALERIAN. I MUST CONFESS I HAVE A SMALL FAVOUR TO ASK...
I WANT TO KEEP MY METAMORPHIC ABILITIES, AND I KNOW THAT TO MAXIMISE THEIR ARTISTIC EFFECT I MUST REMAIN UGLY. BUT SOMETHING'S ALWAYS BOTHERED ME... I HATE EVEN MENTIONING IT...
GO ON, OLD BOY. LET IT ALL OUT. YOU'LL FEEL BETTER.
IT'S MY SMELL... DO YOU THINK YOU COULD DO SOMETHING?
OF COURSE HE CAN – CAN'T YOU?
I BELIEVE SO...
OH, THANK YOU! IN ADVANCE, THANK YOU!
TOUCHING, HUH?
LOVELY!
YOU'RE VERY WELCOME...
50

WHAT NOW?

THE JUMP CIRCUITS ARE STUCK. RETURN TRIP TO 20TH-CENTURY EARTH — CAN'T CHANGE IT...

HOW WERE AUDIENCES BACK THEN?

YOU SHOULD BE QUITE A HIT.

HAVE YOU THOUGHT OF AN AGENT?

NOT A KATUBIAN, I HOPE?...

OF COURSE NOT! BUT OUR OLD FRIEND MR ALBERT HAS MANY CONTACTS. HE'LL KNOW WHAT TO DO.

WE OK LEAVE!... NOT LOTS ROCKS HERE!

ANCIENT TERRA! A SOPHISTICATED PLACE WE USED TO DREAM OF ON OUR HORRIBLE PLANET BROMN. MY DEAR VALERIAN AND LAURELINE, MEETING YOU WAS A RARE PLEASURE!

WE'RE ABOUT TO MAKE THE JUMP, EVERYONE! IT COULD BE ROUGH, AND I'M NOT ENTIRELY SURE WHERE WE'LL ARRIVE. STRAP IN!

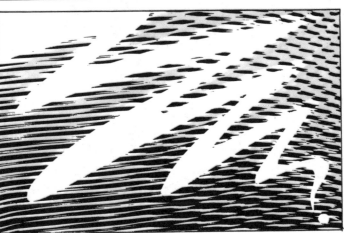

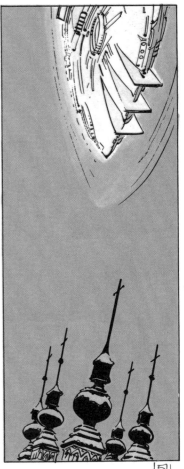

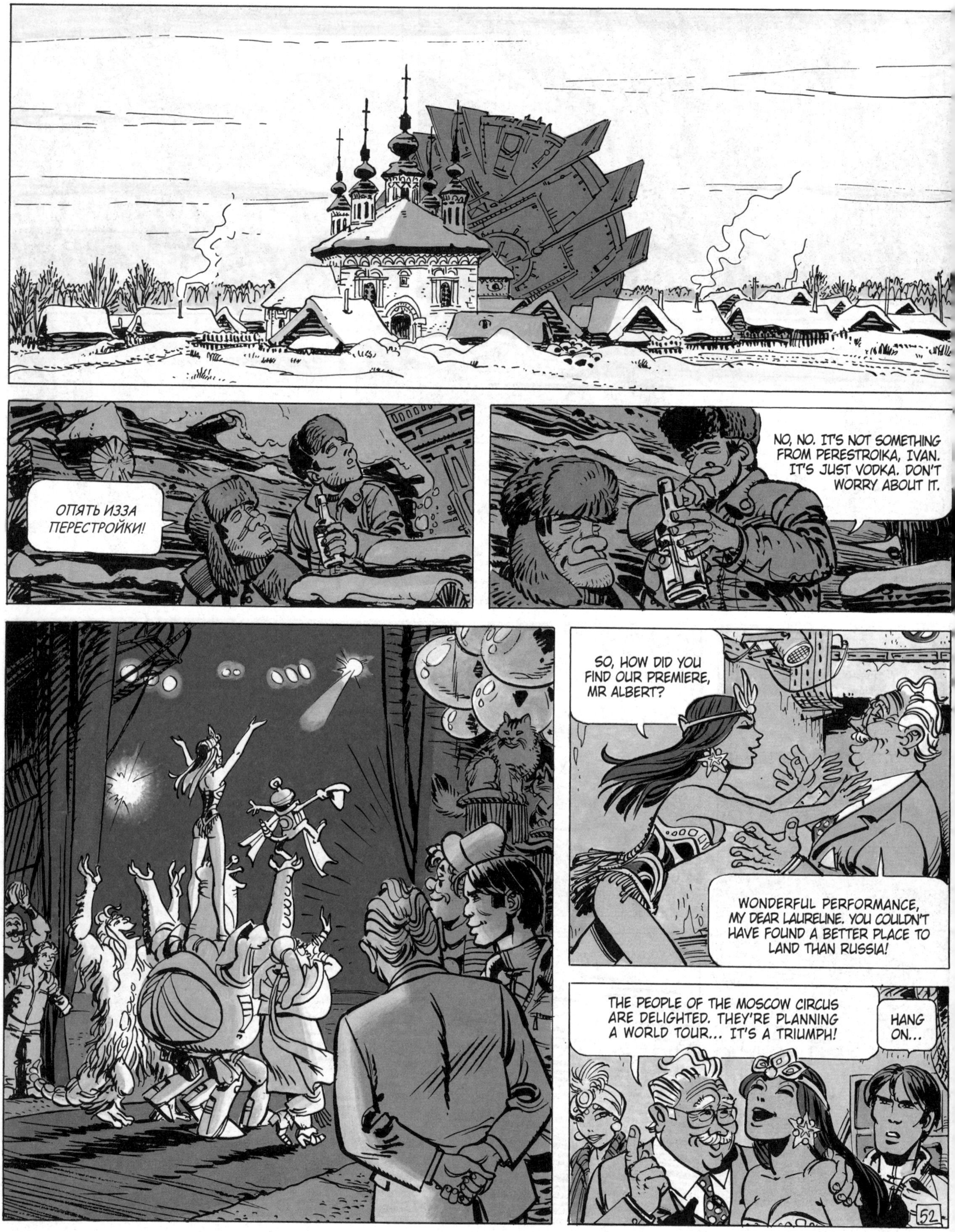
ОПЯТЬ ИЗЗА ПЕРЕСТРОЙКИ!
NO, NO. IT'S NOT SOMETHING FROM PERESTROIKA, IVAN. IT'S JUST VODKA. DON'T WORRY ABOUT IT.
SO, HOW DID YOU FIND OUR PREMIERE, MR ALBERT?
WONDERFUL PERFORMANCE, MY DEAR LAURELINE. YOU COULDN'T HAVE FOUND A BETTER PLACE TO LAND THAN RUSSIA!
THE PEOPLE OF THE MOSCOW CIRCUS ARE DELIGHTED. THEY'RE PLANNING A WORLD TOUR... IT'S A TRIUMPH!
HANG ON...
52

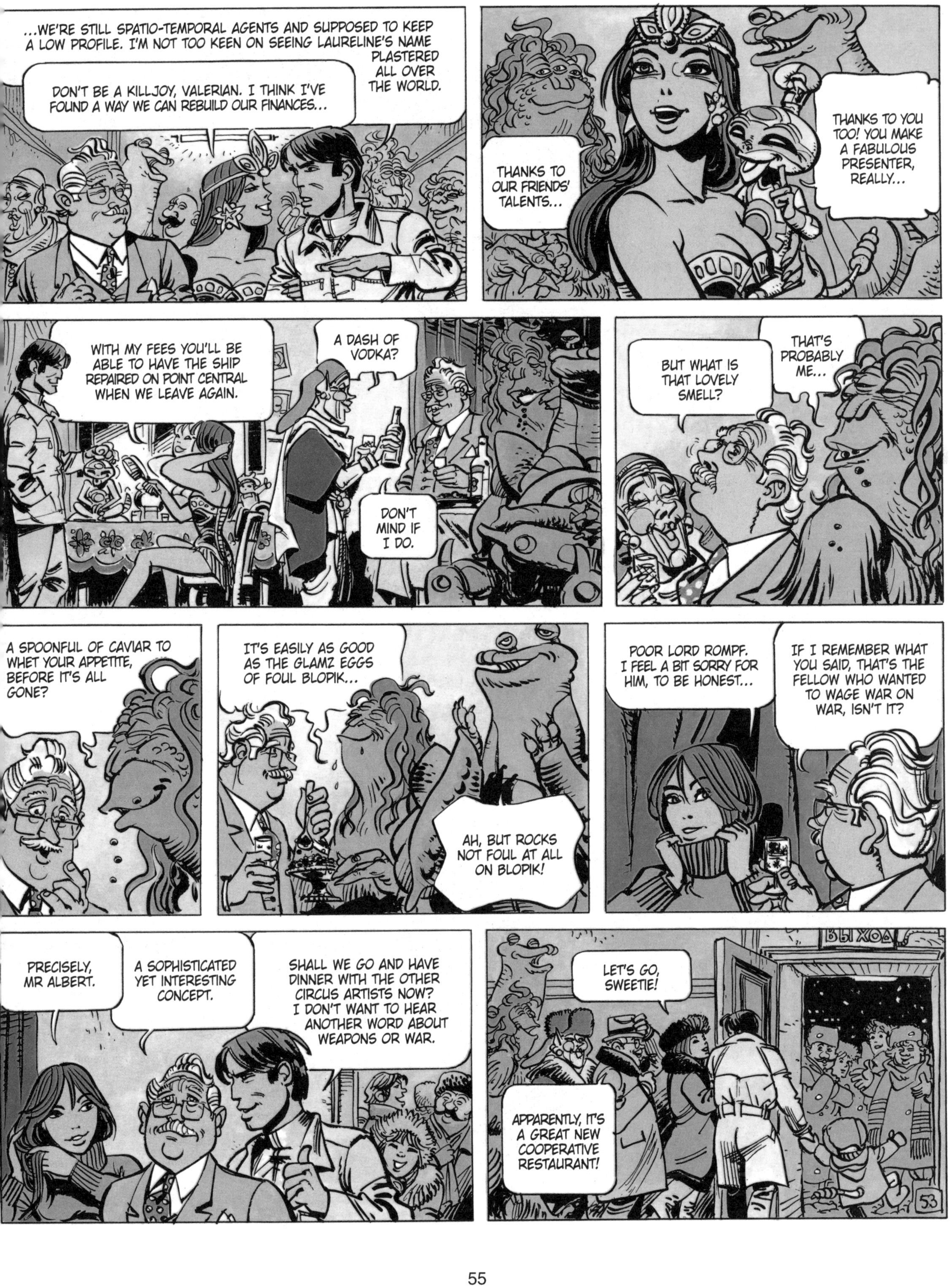
...WE'RE STILL SPATIO-TEMPORAL AGENTS AND SUPPOSED TO KEEP A LOW PROFILE. I'M NOT TOO KEEN ON SEEING LAURELINE'S NAME PLASTERED ALL OVER THE WORLD.
DON'T BE A KILLJOY, VALERIAN. I THINK I'VE FOUND A WAY WE CAN REBUILD OUR FINANCES...
THANKS TO OUR FRIENDS' TALENTS...
THANKS TO YOU TOO! YOU MAKE A FABULOUS PRESENTER, REALLY...
WITH MY FEES YOU'LL BE ABLE TO HAVE THE SHIP REPAIRED ON POINT CENTRAL WHEN WE LEAVE AGAIN.
A DASH OF VODKA?
DON'T MIND IF I DO.
BUT WHAT IS THAT LOVELY SMELL?
THAT'S PROBABLY ME...
A SPOONFUL OF CAVIAR TO WHET YOUR APPETITE, BEFORE IT'S ALL GONE?
IT'S EASILY AS GOOD AS THE GLAMZ EGGS OF FOUL BLOPIK...
AH, BUT ROCKS NOT FOUL AT ALL ON BLOPIK!
POOR LORD ROMPF. I FEEL A BIT SORRY FOR HIM, TO BE HONEST...
IF I REMEMBER WHAT YOU SAID, THAT'S THE FELLOW WHO WANTED TO WAGE WAR ON WAR, ISN'T IT?
PRECISELY, MR ALBERT.
A SOPHISTICATED YET INTERESTING CONCEPT.
SHALL WE GO AND HAVE DINNER WITH THE OTHER CIRCUS ARTISTS NOW? I DON'T WANT TO HEAR ANOTHER WORD ABOUT WEAPONS OR WAR.
ВЫХОД
LET'S GO, SWEETIE!
APPARENTLY, IT'S A GREAT NEW COOPERATIVE RESTAURANT!
53

ОСКОВСКИЙ
ЦИРК
ЛОРЕЛИНА
И ЕЁ ДРУЗЬЯ
!?
ME STAY HERE. CONCRETE A BIT CHEWY, BUT GOOD.
TO WAGE WAR ON WAR, OR NOT TO WAGE WAR ON WAR? THAT IS THE QUESTION.

P. CHRISTIN
J.C. MÉZIÈRES
89-90

THE END

54